# Draíocht Ceoil

## The Sound of Magic in Irish Traditions

# Draíocht Ceoil

## The Sound of Magic in Irish Traditions

Geraldine Moorkens Byrne

London, UK
Washington, DC, USA

First published by Moon Books, 2026
Moon Books is an imprint of Collective Ink Ltd.,
Unit 11, Shepperton House, 89 Shepperton Road, London,
N1 3DF office@collectiveinkbooks.com
www.collectiveinkbooks.com
www.moon-books.net

For distributor details and how to order please visit the 'Ordering' section on our website.



ISBN: 978 1 78535 530 1
978 1 917704 08 3 (ebook)
Library of Congress Control Number: 2025931407



A CIP catalogue record for this book is available from the British Library.

Design: Lapiz Digital Services

UK: Printed and bound by CPI Group (UK) Ltd, Croydon, CR0 4YY
Printed in North America by CPI GPS partners



The manufacturer's authorised representative in the EU for product safety is:
eucomply OÜ - Pärnu mnt 139b-14, 11317 Tallinn, Estonia, hello@ eucompliancepartner.com,
www.eucompliancepartner.com

## What People Are Saying About

# Draíocht Ceoil

*Draíocht Ceoil* is a fascinating deep dive into the power of speech and song, exploring historic and modern uses within Irish folk magic. A must-read book on a subject that can be foundational to magic – and life – yet is too often ignored. I recommend this for anyone who is interested in Irish magical practices or anyone who wants to learn more about the power within our voice and how to harness that intentionally.
**Morgan Daimler**, author of *The Morrigan*

*Draíocht Ceoil: The Sound of Magic in Irish Traditions* is more than just a book. It is a condensed expression of a legacy which Geraldine Byrne, through her exquisite writing, passes on to us – those passionate about Irish cultural heritage and magical traditions.
**Daniela Simina**, author of *Where Fairies Meet*

As both an Irish musician and practitioner of magic, I found Byrne's *Draíocht Ceoil* to be an essential read. This seminal work explores the interwoven tapestry of Ireland's music, tradition, landscape, language and culture, with comprehensive exercises to assist inexperienced and professional readers both in deepening their understanding of and connection to Ireland's culture, and indeed her very soul. Throughout many years of walking the land, living in both urban and rural areas, I was keenly aware of the concepts of 'Brí' and 'Bua', but was unaware that they had specific names which were known to my ancestors. These concepts and many more are explored in depth in Byrne's book. *Draíocht Ceoil* is an engaging and important book for the process of reclaiming and reconnecting with

authentic Irish culture at a time when it is difficult to discern facts from misinformation. Byrne is 'singing over the bones' – the recognisable remnants – of a rich and complex heritage, which comes to life before us, chapter by chapter and page by page.
**Tara Tine**, Diary of a Ditch Witch (YouTube), Performance Artist

*Draíocht Ceoil* is a wonderful symphony of sound and language, beating to the rhythm of the Irish bodhrán for connection to the self, to each other and to the land. Through research, personal experience and a palpable *grá* for her subject, Moorkens Byrne presents the magical power of sound that is within each of us and all around us. A fascinating and practical read for protection and magical workings, steeped in Irish folklore, Irish tradition, Irish language and of course Irish *Ceoil*.
**Pauline Breen**, author of *This Is Brigit*

# Contents

**Also by Geraldine Moorkens Byrne**

Dreams Of Reality, A Collection of Poetry
ISBN 978-1739649654

Dedicated to those who came before, those who will come after and those who are doing the work right now.

# Acknowledgements

Grateful thanks are due to all those who have helped and encouraged the writing of this book, including but by no means limited to Morgan Daimler, Lora O'Brien, Daniela Simina, Mael Brigde and my students. Special thanks to my husband, Mark, for his help and expertise, and to the many musicians who made Charlie Byrne's Music Shop such a wonderful place.

And of course, to my parents Charles and Maria, who preserved and passed on a wonderful legacy.

# Foreword

Through *Draíocht Ceoil: The Sound of Magic in Irish Traditions,* Geraldine Moorkens Byrne introduces the reader to Draíocht Ceoil, the practice of sung magic, a component that features prominently in the Irish magico-spiritual landscape. Draíocht Ceoil is a system in which poetry and music are catalysts for manifesting magically expressed intent. The practice draws its power from the sheer beauty of the Irish language combined with the artistry of Fílidecht, the craft of the ancient Irish poets unmatched in their skill with words. And no one is better qualified for the task of examining and explaining Draíocht Ceoil than historian, musician, teacher and author, Geraldine Moorkens Byrne. As the readers will have the pleasure of discovering, Geraldine is rooted in Dublin's history and music tradition, not only through her passion and profession but also as part of her family's living legacy.

One may be surprised to find out that not long ago, the practice of music magic in Ireland did not have a specific name. There was no unifying term to circulate across the Island for this particular aspect of an otherwise omnipresent practice. Ordinary people and ritual specialists alike have been singing their magic just as they saw their own parents and grandparents doing, who, in turn, had learned from their predecessors. The name Draíocht Ceoil was coined relatively recently, when the practice began to draw attention as a precious part of the Irish cultural heritage.

*Draíocht Ceoil: The Sound of Magic in Irish Traditions* opens up a window for readers to see into a past when magic was part of everyday life. Music and magic pervade many if not all Irish spiritual traditions. The power of music is undeniable: a song can take listeners down memory lane, make them laugh, cry, or give wings to their dreams even if only for a moment.

Such power is by itself magical, and Geraldine herself is a firm believer in the magical power of sound. In the practice of Draíocht Ceoil, Irish sung magic, sound is used to tap into the vast reservoir of magical energy which is then shaped through the usage of words.

Through song, magic has been intentionally embedded into activities such as wool spinning, knitting, even kneading dough. We learn that music magic, or sung magic, Draíocht Ceoil, was performed not only by ordinary people when carrying out mundane tasks but it was also the purview of ritual specialists. Mná Feasa, Women of Knowledge or Wise Women, had the role of both assisting members of their communities and also perpetuating the tradition of sung magic.

Draíocht Ceoil has been transmitted intergenerationally and as the precious heritage that it is, this practice needs to be protected and preserved for future generations. To give the reader a sense of how weighty this responsibility is, Geraldine introduces the social and historical context that led to the near-obliteration of Irish language and culture. While today the Republic of Ireland is no longer subject to colonial oppression, both the Irish language and folk traditions are still in danger. Protecting these is as important as it is urgent. It is inherently human to want to protect things that we hold dear and deem as important to us. To this avail, the author invites the readers to both intellectually understand and practically participate in Draíocht Ceoil.

But the author of *Draíocht Ceoil* doesn't stop at explaining the meaning, history and importance of preserving this practice. Geraldine Moorkens Byrne introduces readers to the nuts and bolts of Draíocht Ceoil inviting them to explore it. Geraldine presents the practice in ways that make it approachable even for people from outside Ireland. However, the word 'accessibility' should not mislead anyone into believing that the practicum section in Draíocht Ceoil is just a collection of quick fixes, pick-and-choose Irish sung charms to be done by rote. Involvement with the practice of Draíocht Ceoil must begin with connecting to Irish culture, both old and new, which is the foundation for learning any kind of native Irish spiritual practice. Throughout the book, Geraldine goes to great lengths to provide guidelines toward practicing Irish sung magic in ways that are respectful toward Irish culture and non-appropriative.

The importance of connecting with Irish spiritual culture cannot be underestimated. Since Draíocht Ceoil is magic that originates in the heart, without feeling the beating heart of Ireland, one cannot feel its magic streaming straight out from their heart. Irish sung magic is not a fossilized item preserved behind glass in a museum, nor is it a relic associated with times long gone. Draíocht Ceoil has grown from ancient roots and its growth is intertwined with the ever-evolving Irish cultural landscape. Geraldine provides readers with all the necessary resources to connect organically with Draíocht Ceoil in its authentic form.

On a mission to keep alive the flame of Irish spiritual traditions, Geraldine Moorkens Byrne wrote this book to draw awareness to the ever-ancient yet ever-new practice of Draíocht Ceoil. Music speaks to the soul and music as a language knows no frontiers. Sung magic is life-affirming. Draíocht Ceoil is bursting with zest for life, an expression of the ultimate determination to break through obstacles that cannot be cleared otherwise.

From *Draíocht Ceoil: The Sound of Magic in Irish Traditions*, we learn that song and words are both things of beauty and power-weapons. In writing this book, Geraldine Moorkens Byrne teaches us how, through words woven into melody, we can magic our way onward, stay undeterred on our paths, rekindle the flame of hope and find power within our own hearts.

**Daniela Simina**, author of *Where Fairies Meet: Parallels between Irish and Romanian Fairy Traditions, A Fairy Path: The Memoir of a Young Fairy Seer in Training,* and *"Fairy Herbs for Fairy Magic: A Practical Guide to Fairy Herbal Magic"*.

# Preface

This book is a long time in the writing, inspired by both a lifetime working with musical instruments and musicians, and a life dedicated to understanding and preserving Irish Folk Magic traditions. The tradition dearest to my heart is that of Draíocht Ceoil, the use of music and sound to create magic. How I came to this path was both through family heritage and personal interest.

My family tradition of music started with my great grandfather, David Byrne, who was a piano tuner, and expert in restoring pianos, harps and harpsichords (already an endangered species by his day). He worked in the mid nineteenth century, in Dublin's Northside. My grandfather, Charles David Byrne, continued the family business, taking over in the 1920s. He was a Master of restoration (pianos and harps) a skill he taught my father, who in turn expanded into stringed orchestral instruments. Dad's love for the violin in particular earned him a place in the memories – and hearts – of several generations of Irish music lovers. With the help of my mother, a businesswoman in her own right, he took the music shop to a new generation and cemented its reputation for excellence. I was the fourth generation in my family to work in the family music shop and did so for almost thirty years starting in 1992. I took over in the early noughties until I retired in 2021.

The shop may have started life on the Northside, but its final move to the Southside in the 1920s made it a part of the fabric of Dublin city. The building it occupied in Lower Stephen Street had been in my dad's maternal family for many years prior to the music shop. My great grandfather, James Monahan, lived and worked there and his daughter, Christina, married my grandfather Charlie Byrne. Under James, the premises was a barber shop before the newlyweds took over. Between both businesses, my family was at the centre of Dublin life – and history – for almost two hundred years.

The music shop in particular witnessed the Rising, War of Independence and Civil War, with both the Monahans and Byrnes playing their part. Over time, Charles Byrne Music became a part of the cultural landscape from the world of classical music to the folk revival of the sixties.

As children my siblings and I had a privileged childhood in many ways, although money was almost universally tight in the seventies and eighties in Ireland. But we had music, loving parents, holidays around Ireland. My parents sacrificed and saved so that we could go on school trips abroad and have a solid education. My sisters and I went to third level education, which would have seemed far beyond the wildest dreams of my ancestors. Music, and musical instruments, were the reason we had all these things, through the hard work and talent of both my parents.

My father was a collector of stories and having spent large amounts of his childhood in Wicklow, as well as in Dublin, he was a font of ghost stories, superstitions, tall tales, piseógs and more. A love of music was in his DNA, and music played a role in many of the stories he told us. These ranged from tales of the haunting music of the Sí luring the unwary from their paths, to the story of Piper Nash, a famous Irish Traveller musician, who rescued my great uncle Peter when he was a wanted man (long story short, Peter tried to shoot a landlord during the land wars in the late nineteenth century. If you knew the landlord, you would side with Peter).

As a child I listened avidly, as a teenager I rolled my eyes and finally, thankfully, as an adult I knew enough to ask him to repeat the tales and write them down.

Dad's mother was held to have "the sight," although that sounds more dramatic than the reality. She was by all accounts an unassuming woman, industrious and devoted to her husband.

She died in childbirth, and my father's knowledge of her came second hand from those who knew her, but he was proud of the many stories told around Dublin about her. Even in the 1990s, there were people who still remembered her – I was working in the shop one day when two women called in, explaining that they were over from the UK, and had come to see the street their parents had lived on. Most of the landmarks they had been told about were gone, except Charlie Byrne's Music Shop on Lower Stephen Street.

"Tell me," one of them said, "would you know about the family here?"

When I explained I was a Byrne, they excitedly told me how Christina Byrne, nee Monahan, had predicted that their parents would meet and how. Their mother had been "disappointed" in love, and in no mood to entertain another suitor, until Christina told her she would "turn a corner and meet the love of her life." Their mother rolled her eyes, stomped off in high dudgeon, turned the corner into Aungier Street, and knocked down a nice man carrying parcels. He took one look at her, and that was it for him. They were married soon after.

Christina's mother Elisabeth Hayes had as long-lasting a reputation but for very different reasons. She was held to have the evil eye, and few wanted to cross her. Whether she really was bad or whether she was a strong and opinionated woman in an unforgiving era, I have often wondered, but the stories about her were consistent. If you had something she wanted, you either gave it up willingly or risked it being spoiled. My grandfather, whom my mother says never spoke ill of anyone, was adamant that she had the "hard word," i.e. a tendency to curse, and ill-wish.

There was a magic too, in the way all three generations of Byrne men could manipulate wood, coax sound from the most battered, neglected instruments and bring them back to life. My father collected beautiful volumes on violin repair, on early instruments and their varnishes, and on tools for instrument making, yet without reference to any of them he could place a soundpost within a fraction of an inch of perfect sound conductivity and pare a bridge into perfect dimensions. I once saw him restore an old violin that was handed in a shoe box-Hurricane Charley in 1986 hit the owner's house and flooded it, the man's precious heirloom violin floating around in its case for a week. When he opened it, every piece of it had separated from the rest. It was a heap of ribs, belly, back, neck and assorted fittings. My dad sighed, shook his head, and wandered off, carrying the box like it housed a puppy. He was talking to it. I wrote a docket, put "ring for updates," where the collection date should have been, and the owner left, begging Dad to "at least try," to save it. A month later, my father handed me a handsome violin, the wood gleaming.

"Tune it up," he said, "and we'll see how it holds."

The owner cried when he saw it – it was in better shape than before the flood. The bottom of that man's house was destroyed, his furniture rotten, photographs ruined and paperwork a sodden mess. But his violin survived to play on, and there was magic in that too.

When we talk of Draíocht Ceoil, we talk not only of sound but of our attachment to it, to music, to familiar voices, to the instruments we play and to the memories it carries. Draíocht Ceoil is not only a traditional folk practice, but an intrinsic part of Irish heritage, culture and society. In a wider context it is a universal practice, consciously or unconsciously uniting us with every era and culture whose own music conjured up dreams and aspirations. There ways in which Draíocht Ceoil affects our lives are myriad and complex, and they enrich us.

My personal journey brought me to a fascination with the way we Irish place such emphasis on the magical properties of sound. I am a poet, and I operate in the spiritual tradition of the *Filí*. My practice has always been rooted in the understanding of the power of words, of sound, and in the ability of sound to create change in our physical reality. In short, like the poets of old, I believe that sound is magic.

Among the fun and madness of dealing with musicians all day long and the equally rewarding chaos that is life among poets, there has always been that constant melody – the sweet, wild strains that come on a moonlit night, or whisper their song on the wind. The music of the Sí, the echoes of songs that are even older. I was delighted to teach a class for the Irish Pagan School on Rosc poetry, which led to a class on Draíocht Ceoil. The deep interest and connection students of both classes displayed led to this book – an attempt to share a practice that is as old as Ireland itself, and an intrinsic part of our culture.

And a note of warning – if you are reading this hoping for a quick fix, easy guide to becoming an expert in Draíocht Ceoil, please close the book and walk away quietly. There is a lifetime of work and exploration to do in every discipline in the Irish traditions and even then, there is always more to learn. No one authority is the be all and end all. Folk magic in particular is an intuitive and individual practice, albeit bounded by culture and tradition. One person will be highly technical, another will operate instinctively. The first lesson in any discipline of learning is to accept that we can never know it all.

There's a lot of background information in the first few chapters that will help you understand the cultural context and history of this practice. However, I have included practical exercises, explanations and suggestions for you to try throughout the book as well as some outlines and exercises at the end. The more you incorporate an awareness of sound and its energy into your daily life, the more you will get out of the tradition of Draíocht Ceoil. It is also important to have some fun with it. At its heart, it is a joyful practice and one that encourages self-expression. So, lift your voice, bang a pot lid and make some noise.

It's magic.

## Chapter 1

# An Overview

> *"Tír gan teanga, tír gan anam. A country without a language is a country without a soul."*
>
> Pádraig Pearse 1879-1916

We Irish are famous for our music, our poetry, and our skill with the written and spoken word. Even in a language not our own, imposed on us by brutal conquest and colonialism, we excel in creating our own rhythms and coining our own phrases. We created Hiberno-English from the rhythms and structure of Irish, mixed with Elizabethan English. They took our language from us, and we revenged ourselves by being better at theirs than they were.

But there is nothing, no sound on earth, sweeter than the song of your own people. Ireland in common with many indigenous, post-colonial nations, struggles now with our native language. Our *teanga náisiúnta* (national language) is constantly in danger, from our own education system as well as external forces. It is not alone in needing protection. Our folk traditions and folk magic, our heritage from Old Irish society, Brehon law, Druidic legacies of language and File traditions all need nurturing. The influence of modern imports like Wicca, Neo-Druidism, eclectic new age fads, and cultural appropriation as well as a domestic problem of internalized colonialism, have all contributed to the danger.

At the end of the book (in the Valuable Resources section) I have listed books, websites and groups that are reliable educational sources for authentic Irish tradition. Priority is given to indigenous sources. Failing to centre Irish voices is in itself a form of colonialism. There are definitely some excellent non-Irish resources e.g. Morgan Daimler and some absolute hokum written by Irish people but a rule of thumb, look first for well-researched, indigenous sources. Read the primary source material where possible (much of it is available online now).

Draíocht Ceoil is a system of knowledge, made up of poetry and music. We can identify Draíocht Ceoil in various practices throughout Irish history, a thread woven throughout our culture. The ability to play music was especially valued in Irish society. Music could change how you felt, music could lead to liminal spaces. People knew it, like they knew that milk soured in hot weather or the best way to cook potatoes. It is important to remember that when a living tradition is recorded and codified, it's really just a snapshot of a moment in time. The practices about which I write were a normal part of everyday life for centuries. It is the same with all Irish folk magic. People went to mass, placated the Sidhe, lit candles to Holy Mary, sang while they spun and tried to tell the future by the fireside. None of this exists in a vacuum.

But to preserve and pass on these traditions, to enable those outside the practice to explore it, we need to codify it to some extent and present it in an orderly fashion. This includes understanding where it stands in a cultural context – Irish traditions are living traditions and should not be divorced from their roots. To this end, let's explore some of the cultural background to the tradition.

In every community there were those whose role it was to facilitate magical practices and beliefs. Echoes of them are embedded in the National Folklore collection with stories of men and women held to have "the cure," or stories of musicians of local renown whose abilities were otherworldly. One enduring character is that of the *Bean Feasa* (a woman of knowledge or wise woman) who stood between the community and the Otherworld – women like P na Lí, or Biddie Early. They knew the remedy for both mundane ills and supernatural misfortunes.

Often problems were attributed to some interaction with the Sidhe, the Good Neighbours, or some infringement of the taboos surrounding liminal spaces. In one example, *The Girl from Sherkin Island,* the local *Bean Feasa* cured a child of loss of speech by diagnosing that her house was built in the wrong place, and her father had had an interaction with "a red haired woman of the Harnedys" (presumably supernatural) who hit him with her stick.

In Arklow, we see the *Bean Feasa* pitted against the local priest who condemned her and told the people not to believe in her.

> *"One day the priest was going down the street and his horse fell and no matter what the priest or anyone else done they could not get it up. The wise woman happened to be going down the street and she came upon the scene, and she shook her apron and the horse jumped up. The priest never said anything bad about her again."*[1]

The powers of the *Bean Feasa* were sometimes described in terms of trances and fits, for example, a story of Joan Grogan, a wise woman from Clare, who was "in her fits" at the bedside of a sick man when his nephew arrived. Without letting the boy speak she admonished him for kicking a piece of turf along the road, saying that if he found anything on the road, to "pass it by and leave it behind you."[2]

The power and status of a wise woman in the community is easily seen by the many references to them in folk stories. Parts of the country still cherish memories of the women who held their communities together, and while we tend to associate them with rural areas, urban communities had their own. In the tenements of Dublin, Limerick or Cork, or among the Claddagh area of Galway the powers of clairvoyance, cures, *piseógs* and magic were all attributed to those considered to be wise women. While the terminology may vary, the role remained the same.

But even here we do not see some homogeneous tradition or secret cult – this was just a part and parcel of community life in Ireland. This was not a role with initiations, and rituals, but a skill-based job, which was valued because it was of service.

On the flip side of the *Bean Feasa,* we find stories of women considered "outside" the norms of society. They are held responsible for minor mischief such as interfering with the churning of butter, or stealing milk from cows, sometimes in the guise of a hare.[3] Widows, even those popular in their community, were feared for their ability to curse, something that was seen a lot in folk stories in the nineteenth century, during the ravages of The Great Hunger, and later during the land wars, in an era when the death of the husband routinely meant eviction for the widow and children. Widows were associated with several forms of magic, from the Widows Curse to the significance of widow's keys in divination.[4]

These stories reflect the precarious situation of a *Bean Feasa,* how easily one might slip from valued to feared, depending on the narrative. In addition to this role, those with creative talents were given special and magical status in their communities. When an individual or family was associated with music, they were accorded an elevated status. If combined with a reputation for supernatural abilities, they were even more valued.

This has its roots in the Old Irish traditions of Harpists and *Filí* being among the elite of society, which we will explore in more detail in later chapters. In the folklore and folk magic of the last few centuries, the ability to create entertainment is not only an important part of social and communal life, but it also becomes a vehicle for political expression and a way to preserve cultural identity and knowledge. Likewise, in a population denied access to legal or medical systems, magic becomes even more important, a way of achieving some level of justice or protection and a way of navigating the traditional belief in the Otherworld.

The Christianization of Ireland was a long and syncretic process that not only incorporated indigenous beliefs into a Christian framework but also in turn, recorded and preserved these older beliefs. The Irish were both devout Catholics, in the teeth of widespread persecution of that religion, and at the same time harboured firmly held and complex beliefs in the Sidhe, the Otherworld, old Gods turned saints, beasties, ghosts and more. As part of this cultural tapestry, Draíocht Ceoil exists in one form or another throughout this history, not always called by any formal name or codified in a system, but as an integral part of everyday life.

Among musicians, and those who create or maintain instruments, we see a special relationship with folk magic, and the community. There existed a belief in the power of music and in its association with the Otherworld, as well as pride in their ability to use music for the communal good. The longer the association within a family, the more apparent and overt this becomes. In my own family, I can trace the beliefs and practices of the older generations in Wicklow, in the early 1800s, through the migration of my particular branch of the Byrnes to Dublin, in the mid nineteenth century, mainly through the ability of my father to pass on these traditions. My Dad spent summers in Wicklow, in a rural community, and the rest of the year in the urban environment, and carried with him the stories of both, passing them on to the next generation. He had endless tales of ghosts, of hungry grass, of strange visitors and of the fairy tree that stood on his family's land. He carried superstitions and nuggets of wisdom – sometimes practical and sometimes esoteric – and he had a knack for weaving them into a narrative. His talent in making and repairing instruments placed him at the top of his art, and I do not exaggerate when I say his ability to restore a broken instrument was nothing short of magical.

Across Ireland, we see an abundance of talent in making instruments and composing and playing music. I will discuss in depth the special position of music in Irish culture, but for now, it is worth noting that in few other nations is music so intrinsic a part of life as in Ireland.

## Where to Start?

So, with that all said, here we are, staring at the past and hoping to bring out enough of its secrets to be able to practice a living, vibrant tradition of music, sound and magic. On our side is the fact that it is a living tradition; one that adapted and survived despite the destruction of the society in which it flourished. There are several reasons why it clung to life. Firstly, the fact that many aspects of the old society in which it is rooted survived until its decline in the Elizabethan period and further destruction in Cromwell's era. Secondly, the existence of books of legal and societal tracts as well as mythological and spiritual texts from medieval Ireland. These contain precious insights into poetic forms such as the Rosc, into the association of music and magic, and the culture that created our rich magical heritage.

The strength of Irish culture played a part as well, the ability as a people to absorb and adapt our heritage and convert it to folk practice. While the British castigated us as "superstitious," our ancestors kept nuggets of belief and practice alive, embedding them in everyday life. This is not to pretend an unbroken, secret tradition – what survived were echoes, which require scholarship and research to link to their Old Irish roots – but it is something to admire in our largely "illiterate",[5] poor and oppressed ancestors.

Draíocht Ceoil is literally, "Music Magic" but a better definition of the practice itself would be, "the inherent magic or power in sound, including words and music." We are going to look at the origins of Draíocht Ceoil, including the status of music in Old Irish society, the magic and power associated with it and its links with both deity and magic. We will also learn about the File, the Old Irish order of poets, their use of language and their understanding of the power in sound. We will trace and explore the associations of music and magic in the folk traditions of Ireland, and the ways in which music and sound, including words, were used in Folk Magic. Music has always been used to express spirituality and is a powerful tool for journeying and prayer and we will explore this. There will be a special section on practical applications but there are also exercises given throughout the book that you can work with.

## Why Choose Draíocht Ceoil?

Time and again, we remind people that when they talk about Irish magical or spiritual practices that they are accessing a living tradition. We don't just reconstruct our heritage, out of dry, arid history. Nor do we construct it from Unsupported Personal Gnosis (UPG). UPG has a role in any individual practice, but anything that is UPG should be clearly labeled as such. This is the approach I will take in this book.

As a nation, we live our traditions. Many Irish people will recognize practices in this book as things that have always been done. For others, there is a sense of homecoming and that is very bittersweet. We have a legacy of colonial brutality to thank for the fact that many people have been denied their own language, history and tradition. If you are reading this from outside Ireland, you too may recognize some of the practices, without realizing that you had felt that connection. Indeed, many who have no obvious connection to Ireland but are drawn to its culture and heritage find that the practice of Draíocht Ceoil speaks to their soul. Music and sound are universal languages.

The practice of Draíocht Ceoil is above all, a joyous one. Not that every situation is easily resolved by a bit of positive thinking – we're not Disney characters bursting into song before a happy ending – but it is a life affirming path and encourages us to be heard. It makes us aware of the song of the universe, and the music in everyday life. It roots us in the present, by making us conscious and aware, but it also connects us to the past and helps us shape the future.

And it can be a lot of fun. Nothing like singing out loud or banging a pot or pretending to be a rock star guitarist to raise the spirits. Sometimes all the magic we need is to laugh. You do not need to be a musician, although a love of music is essential. If you can sing or play an instrument, you will find that skill very useful, but it is not a requirement. Nor is a background in music theory, or formal education in music in any way. We are all capable of making sound.

## Who Can Practice Draíocht Ceoil?

Music is a powerful tool and a universal one. When it comes to cultural appropriation, it can be difficult to know where common human experience ends and indigenous, protected culture starts. Sometimes the line is clear e.g. when a community steals from another community whom they historically oppress. But if you love Irish music and history and just want to join in – is that flattery or theft? If you have some Irish heritage, are you more entitled to access Irish heritage? When musicians from diverse cultures play together, it is an act of community and shared human culture; but does that confer ongoing permission to outsiders to use indigenous folk songs?

The same questions apply to Irish magical and spiritual traditions. There is no easy answer but as a rule, Draíocht Ceoil is open to those who learn and respect it. But that means cultivating a deep connection, not a cursory or eclectic one. You cannot divorce Irish traditions from their roots. You cannot understand one tiny part of them and claim to be authentic. You cannot read a book (even one as fabulous as this) and then claim to be an expert.

If you are willing to understand, learn, and practice – welcome aboard. If you want a quick fix, once again I beg you, close the book and step away quietly.

And as an aside, please remember that no matter how many Irish ancestors you have, nationality is not a matter of DNA. People who emigrate into Ireland, live here, and choose this country as their home, are Irish, regardless of the colour of their skin or where they and their families hail from originally. Irish traditions are not to be used as a basis for biological racism.

In a way, Irish indigenous traditions can be said to be semi-closed. Because we acknowledge the ties many have to the country and culture due to emigration, we expect outside interest. But we are protective of the culture we are fighting so hard to preserve and the magical traditions we are recording for future generations. We spend a lot of time and energy seeking out the authentic, only to see it stolen and repackaged into a new age, social media friendly, mishmash of appropriation.

I hope that readers will be inspired not only to incorporate Draíocht Ceoil into their lives but to respect the tradition that created it, and to dig deeper into the history and practices.

## Irish or English?

Our national language is Irish and there can be no question that the beauty and power of the older literary forms, especially the Rosc, are best expressed and experienced in Irish. But the brutal reality is that many Irish people, including myself, speak English as our first language. This is not a new development. The use of Irish declined sharply across the country in the mid nineteenth century as the Penal Laws confirmed English as the language of economics, politics and law. Ireland does business with the world, and English is one of the most widely used languages. Even if we could revert to being a majority of Irish speakers, we would still have to use English daily. It's just reality.

Still, learning even a little Irish is highly recommended. We do the best we can with the tools we have. Even in English, the beauty of Irish forms and poetic structure shine through. Hiberno-English is a recognized language, and as many of the tools of Draíocht Ceoil rely on sound, rather than words, once you understand how to use sound, it can be effective in any language.

At the back of this work, you'll find a glossary of Irish terms. There are words that really cannot be translated into English, like *"Brí" "Bua"* and *"Rosc"* but where possible I've provided at least an explanation and a pronunciation guide.

## Practical Application

There will be practical examples and exercises all the way through this book, and a section devoted to the practical use of Draíocht Ceoil. I heavily encourage you to do the exercises that are given in the body of the work, to build up a solid foundation before moving on to the examples and outlines given in the last chapters. Draíocht Ceoil is a skill that should be integrated into your life rather than a sterile exercise to be done once a week.

## Religion

People often conflate the practice of witchcraft with Neo-pagan religion. Irish traditions of word, and music magic, are not religious. They are arts, and skill based. Trying to impose some kind of religious structure retrospectively would be inauthentic, and while individuals may choose to mix religion and magic in their own practice, this should never be seen as somehow implying that it is traditional. Folk magic from early medieval to modern times were part of daily life for Catholic, church-going people. That is not to say that practicing Draíocht Ceoil cannot be part of your spiritual practice; it can, see Chapter 9 Draíocht Ceoil and Spirituality. But its primary use is as a magical tool.

## Draíocht

There is no one true definition of how to do magic in an Irish tradition, and even among Irish practitioners there will be huge differences in approach. You will find some who do approach magic as a form of religious work. You will find some who work with different aspects of Irish traditions from the Sidhe to the practices of blood magic. None of us can claim to be the final authority.

This is my way of working, based on traditional folk practices, and on the work of those who went before me. The most important aspect in Draíocht Ceoil is knowing that magical energy is a natural, neutral energy. It occurs in nature – *Brí* is the energy of wild places, and *Bua* is the energy a place gains through human usage. We can tap into it, and one of the best ways to do so is by "tuning in" to the sound energy all around us. We then use sound to refine, amplify and aim that magical energy (all this will be explored in detail in later chapters).

Music was a ubiquitous part of daily life and holds an extremely strong place still in Irish society. Small wonder that it is part of folk magic too, and one that could be seamlessly incorporated into everyday tasks.

I mentioned this before, but Irish traditions are not Wicca. This means words like coven, rede, rule of three, quarters, etc. have no relevance. Hexing and malediction are a valid part of Irish tradition, rooted in the ancient practices of Satire and the rights of the Irish *Filí*. There is no concept of punishment for using magic, only rules about breaking taboos, being rude or intrusive in liminal spaces or in dealings with the Sidhe. Generally speaking, our ancestors display a robust attitude towards all disciplines of folk magic. Hexing is a valid tool for certain situations.

One thing Irish traditions agree on is that a solid grounding in placing boundaries, protecting yourself, and understanding the ramifications of all your actions are necessities before attempting to practice.

Consent is also an important, if perhaps modern, requirement. Sending healing, protection or similar without asking may be well-meaning but you have no idea of the ramifications of your energy input. And people are entitled to their autonomy – your approval of their actions is not required. Whenever this issue is raised, someone inevitably asks how Hexing can fit into this? The answer is simple; you decide to hex if and only if you are sure of your rights, and of the necessity of hexing. Hexing doesn't require consent, any more than defending yourself against a physical attack requires that you check with your attacker if they're okay with you punching them back. Apart from hexing, in the normal course of things, one thinks about the rights of the other person.

## Poetic Language

When combined into music, sound can have a profound effect. When this is then combined with powerful words or vocal sounds, it becomes even more effective. This is an ancient concept in Ireland. Quite a lot is known about the use of language by the poetic class; most notably the use of one word to convey many meanings and the association of many things with one word.

The ancient text, *The Colloquy of the Two Sages* gives us a taste of the complexity of poetic language. The extraordinary exchanges between Ferchertne and Néde show off the secret meanings of words, designed to be understood by the elite, excluding the majority. Consider one of the opening sallies between the older Ferchertne and the young challenger, Néde. Ferchertne asks Néde for his credentials with *"A question, O instructing lad, whence hast thou come?"* Néde answers by invoking imagery of youth and freshness and in turn asks the same question.

Ferchertne replies:

32. *"Not hard (to say): along the columns of age,*
33. *along the streams of Galion (Leinster),*
34. *along the Elfmound of Nechtan's wife*
35. *along, the forearm of Nuada's wife,*
36. *along the land of the sun (science),*
37. *along the dwelling of the moon,*
38. *along the young one's navel-string."*
(Stokes, 1905)[6]

Never since has an elder smacked down a junior with more aplomb. *"I was doing this before you were a twinkle in your Da's eye,"* we Dubliners would say. But this is more than just a sharp exchange. The language used conveys multiple meanings to an educated audience. The *Filí* elevated words, chants and extemporaneous verse with the use of harp, drum and reed to serve a variety of purposes. Requirements to obtain the position of *Filí* involved both esoteric and practical knowledge. Practical applications included memorizing the different medicinal properties of herbs, names of trees and plants, and politically useful knowledge such as regional oral histories, cultural customs, and stories of heroes, especially ones linked to their patrons by cultural or genealogical connections. Other requirements involved memorizing 10,000 poems, and learning 300 secret languages, such as the Ogham script, itself a system of knowledge linking various items to one symbol much like the multilayered meaning poets attached to words.

In modern folk magic over the last four hundred years, the essence of Draíocht Ceoil is the belief that some sounds carry inherent power. A hum at a certain pitch can be as effective as two paragraphs of carefully chosen words, if you know what you are doing. The beauty of this practice is that there is a tool for every situation, be it a word, a poem, or a passage of music.

The applications are also wide ranging, from healing to hexing, for personal issues as well as large, public issues of social import.

While its roots are visible in the Old Irish past, Draíocht Ceoil evolved into an important modern folk tradition. Nonsense words, extemporaneous singing or chanting, keening and laments and a body of superstitions and beliefs about fairy music, are both echoes of the distant past and part of a vibrant, living practice. While our ancestors may have forgotten the origins of these practices, they carried them with them through societal upheaval, emigration, famine and war.

During most of Ireland's history, folk magic was practiced very much within the framework of society, with the wise woman both rival and peer of the Priest and Doctor. Catholicism was the order of the day, and folk traditions lived alongside incense and altar.

## Sound as Power

The basis of Draíocht Ceoil is simple. Sound resonates, and the energy of sound affects things. This is both an observable scientific phenomenon and a magical truth. If you understand the following principles, you can manipulate sound to effect change in this reality.

In Irish Mythology there is evidence of the three realms, Land Sea and Sky (e.g. in *The Tain*, an Old Irish poem) While various interpretations of this exist, within the tradition I practice these are interpreted as three realities: to whit, this physical reality; the Otherworld; and the inner landscape of the soul. Imrammic meditation can help access, align and harness the three. Sound magic plays a vital role in using magical energy in any or all of these realities.

In Draíocht Ceoil we have five Principles of Magical Energy.

**Principle 1**: Magic is a naturally occurring energy. It exists in nature, as a raw material.

**Principle 2**: Magical energy is expressed in two ways. Firstly *Brí,* which is the energy of wild places, inherent energy and secondly, *Bua* which is the energy a place gains through human use. A place can have a mix of both energies, but one will usually be dominant.

**Principle 3**: This energy can be accessed effectively using sound. You need to practice tuning in to magical energy. Meditation and journeying can help develop the ability to sense it, but sound is the main tool we will be using.

**Principle 4**: Once you can recognize the type of energy in a given place, *Brí* or *Bua,* and can tap into it using sound, you now have the ability to harness using several techniques. These include humming, chanting, nonsense words, and other traditional methods.

**Principle 5**: The use of sound has power, and this power can be amplified, honed, and aimed, using words, instruments and percussion (rhythm).

Look at it as a series of building blocks. We need to understand the foundations, then we experiment with different sounds, then we add the spoken word, and explore the various ways in which words can be added to the practice.

Sometimes simple is best, using a simple word or sound. Sometimes you will construct with great attention to pitch, choosing every word carefully, using multiple meanings and layers. Or you'll go somewhere in between and use humming or singing or nonsense words. The beauty of Draíocht Ceoil is that there is a tool for every job.

## Sound Energy

Something we all do without even realizing it is releasing sound energy. Sound energy is produced when an object vibrates causing waves of pressure that travel through a medium, such as air, water, wood, or metal.

Energy is at the basis of all magic, and it can be dressed up or down. Folk magic tends to strip down to the basics. Sound energy is present in everything from the babble of a stream, birds singing or wind rustling trees, right through to the squeal of brakes in a city, buses engines and gates clanging. Draíocht Ceoil is a doorway into the magical energy all around us. This is what makes it so versatile and so embedded in the fabric of everyday life.

## Sound Disorder, Neurodivergence and Misophonia

Sound may be a part of our lives, but it can also be overwhelming. Out of all the cacophony of modern life, how on earth are you supposed to separate out sounds? And considering how overwhelming some of us find noise, why are people with such acute sensitivities to sound so often good at Draíocht Ceoil?

As a misophone, I suffer from a brain disorder that gives me an unusual sensitivity to sound. Any sound, from the rustle of the leaves in a breeze to absolute silence, can either irritate my brain or soothe it. I have to be aware constantly of the presence or absence of sound. My brain is predisposed to tune in and out of sounds, for self-preservation. This is common to many people who experience neuro-divergent relationships with sound energy and being aware of sound is the first step towards understanding Draíocht Ceoil. Isolation and control of sound elements becomes second nature to many. Hyperacusis – a condition where "normal" sound levels appear overly loud and distorted – is generally relatively rare but more common among neurodivergent individuals and those with autoimmune disorders.

It is commonly accepted that neurodivergent individuals experience sound stimuli differently from others. In 8D audio, the sound will go from one earbud to the other when wearing headphones. This makes people feel especially immersed in the experience. It seems that 8D is best for both neurodivergent and neurotypical brains, promoting relaxation, stress relief, and positive mood, and early studies show that neurodivergent people experience it more intensely.

The common perception of neurodivergent processing of sound is that we get overwhelmed and overstimulated by sound and have to withdraw or filter sounds through earplugs. The reality is far more complex and nuanced. It varies from condition to condition, is affected by both misophonia and hyperacusis and can involve complicated processing and emotional or intellectual reactions. For example, some neurodivergent people process more sounds simultaneously than neurotypical people.[7] A 2017 study posited that the reason for this was survival, that the ability to hear and be hyper aware of more sounds than others went hand in hand with the ability to filter out and identify dangerous sounds, or warning sounds, in that mix. People with ADHD can often focus better when listening to music, specifically music with a calming, repetitive rhythm and clear structure.

Misophonia, synesthesia, and anything that makes us inclined to process sound differently can ensure that Draíocht Ceoil makes intuitive sense, by making us more aware of nuances, hidden sounds, and emotional reactions to sound. What may appear at first to be a disadvantage can be in fact, your greatest asset.

## Sound and Emotional Well-being

Various essays and studies emphasis not only the physiological effects of music on the brain but the emotional benefits. Obvious benefits flow from relaxation through music but when we find music or lyrics that express our experiences, it can be a profound moment. In a way, the power of music in spirituality and magic is based on this ability to connect us to our fellow humans and to our own humanity. For any group that is marginalized, it becomes doubly precious.

Music bonds people emotionally, from the fandom for a particular genre or performer to the joy of listening to music with others. We also benefit from performing with others. Neurodivergent conditions such as misophonia are inextricably linked to emotional regulation while studies have shown that sound has both an inherent ability to provoke an immediate emotional reaction and a strong ability to elicit the same through our memories and associations.

Music is used in cinema, advertisements, and social media to elicit the correct emotional response to a scene or product, with great effect. However, sounds that are divorced from chordal tones, sounds such as sirens, notifications, alerts, also provoke a strong emotional response because of our associations. We know a siren means danger, from police cars to air raids. Our ability to attach emotion to sound, as distinct from being emotionally manipulated by sound, is a key factor in Draíocht Ceoil. Individuals will have intense personal attachment to or revulsion to noise. In later chapters, when constructing practical applications of Draíocht Ceoil, bear this in mind. You can personalize a working by understanding this.

## All Sounds Are Not Equal

There is another basic question to be addressed. Are some sounds more magical than others? Or are all sounds equally magical?

Simply put, while all sound is important, some sounds are more magical, more powerful than others. This can manifest in several ways.

If you are in a particular place, it will have its own unique sound. You will need to listen for and tune into that sound. This takes practice and will be one of the first exercises we tackle. You can tap into it and allow yourself to align to its frequency and pitch. You can also attempt to change it. This is the basis of Draíocht Ceoil. Likewise, crowds and individuals emit sound energy, while different pitches have different effects on both people and places. Pitch is a crucial element in creating magical sound.

## Chapter 2

# The Science of Sound

Before we look at sound magic in an Irish tradition, it is important to understand some of the science and evidence behind the practice. Our ancestors had an intuitive understanding of these things but it's always nice when science illustrates how right they were. All the points raised in this chapter are, of course, worthy of study by themselves, if anyone is interested in doing a deep dive. Having a basic idea of them helps to place the practice in a wider context. There's a good reason that music plays such a huge part of cultural life, globally.

### How Sound Affects Us

We are all of us part of the great Universal song. Music is a fundamental expression of reality, a naturally occurring force that unites all life.

In March 2021 NASA released a recording of the Cat's Eye Nebula.[8] Using data collected by the NASA Chandra Xray, they changed the way space-based telescopes interpret data, by creating "Data sonification maps" which changed data into a form that users can hear. They stress it embodies data in a new form without changing the original content.

The data from the Cat's Eye Nebula, where huge clouds of gas and dust form spectacular structures, combined information from Chandra X-rays in the centre, and visible light data from the Hubble telescope. The result is an extraordinary recording of what without hyperbole one could call one of the songs of the Universe.

In their post, NASA explains that the light that is further from the center is transmitted as higher pitches while the brighter light is louder. The X-rays are represented by a harsher sound, while the visible light data sounds smoother, and the circular rings create a constant hum. The rising and falling pitches that can be heard are due to the radar scan passing across the shells and jets in the nebula.

This one, incredible "sound image" is a space age representation of Draíocht Ceoil and is just one image, out of the infinite beauty and variety of the universe. We are a part of this song, and no wonder that from our earliest moments as a species, we have sought to recreate it, in every culture and in every part of this world. Music has united us more than any other concept, even providing a way to communicate where language fails. I have traveled the world, met people without a word of any common language, and we have made music together.

If you do nothing else, look for the Cat's Eye Nebula recording by NASA listed in the notes section and enjoy.

The great power of sound, especially music, lies in its ability to help us articulate common human experience, as well as personal emotion. We know that humans within a community and culture react in remarkably similar ways to the stimulus of music. Crucially it not only expresses but can create emotional and intellectual responses.

Musicologist Deryck Cooke[9] explored the affect that various minor, major, and chromatic scales have on human emotions. For anyone interested in the subject in greater depth his book *The Language of Music* (1989, OUP) is an excellent read, albeit focused on Western composers of the last few hundred years. For our purposes here, the important takeaway is that our emotions can be manipulated by music, can be deliberately affected and changed, and our intellectual processes – how we think about a subject, or action – can be manipulated along with our feelings. When we respond to a piece of music, we often share our feelings of joy or discomfort with the rest of the audience, without necessarily understanding why. But our cultural conditioning tells us that some chords, played in this way, represent joy while other sounds are discordant and show us pathos, fear or anger.

Cooke also sets out how music is a language. I would call it in fact the primary language of humanity. It can convey a huge range of emotions, needs, and opinions without verbalization. It is similar to poetry as an art form and indeed as we consider Draíocht Ceoil, we cannot separate music from poetry. Both use sound energy to affect material change in this physical reality.

One interesting aspect of voice and expression is how the change in voice, at puberty or in gender transition, affects the individual. We are all familiar with the way a boy's voice changes from childhood to manhood, as testosterone kicks in. As the larynx thickens the higher register of notes gives way to deeper, lower pitched notes. For boys who like singing, this is particularly noticeable, but for most boys it's an exciting development that marks a move into adulthood. For others, struggling with gender identity can be a confusing and difficult experience, widening the gap between inner and outward perception of gender.

For adults undergoing gender transition, there is a complex relationship with vocal transition. I know one lady with a beautiful singing voice who had to forgo professional engagements while her voice entered a higher pitch range; a trade-off between achieving the voice that was a more authentic reflection of her Self and retaining her previous professional status as a baritone. The value to her of having her true voice lay beyond finances or career progression.

Because testosterone-based changes to the larynx tend to be permanent, voice therapy is a great tool to help people alter their voice; studies continue into the emotional benefits especially with regard to aiding trans people to be more readily accepted and recognized as their preferred gender.

The therapeutic effects of sound are complex and far reaching. Apart from the general importance of sound, voice, and emotional reaction to music, it has long been recognized that listening to, dancing to and playing music is associated with entering a flow state, defined as a state in which everything except your current activity becomes irrelevant. Flow states are conducive to magical workings, both for attuning to magical energy and for raising it. There are obvious mental health benefits as well, as with meditation and mindfulness techniques.

Studies have shown that music has benefits for health, both mentally and physically, including affecting hormonal levels (including cortisol and testosterone). Music therapy in a medical (as opposed to spiritual) sense is a rapidly expanding field of neuroscience.

## Sound in Nature

When we talk about sound as a language, it is important to remember that this holds true outside the realm of human activity. We do not have a monopoly on communication, and one of the important steps in opening ourselves to Draíocht Ceoil is to understand that we do not stand outside nature. We are part of the animal kingdom, and our fellow creatures use sound in as complex a way as we do. Think of Ostriches, making the weirdest throat noises by puffing out their necks, or the way insects manipulate sound for mating, social recruitment and defense. Human voices become unintelligible at 100 metres (even the loudmouth with the booming voice) whereas elephants can communicate at 10 kilometres. Not only that, but elephants do so by using infrasound, extremely low frequency sound, less than 20 Hertz. We cannot even hear this sound without specialist equipment.

What elephants do on land, whales can do in the sea – without using infrasound. Instead, they communicate over huge distances using sounds within the 40 to 4000 hertz range. Sound travels faster in water than through air. Bats, shrews, birds, and whales all use echolocation, the use of sound for hunting and navigation. This ability enables bats in particular to be nocturnal, and they can produce sounds as high in frequency as 100,000 Hz.

When we are tempted to pat ourselves on the back for our human use of sound, remember that a bat doesn't find itself lost on the side of the road because it took a wrong turning, or an elephant doesn't need a mobile phone to call up its auntie in a different part of the country.

You do not need to be an expert in musicology or neuroscience to understand Draíocht Ceoil. However, understanding some of this provides a solid base for understanding the power of sound.

On a simple, personal level, the sounds of nature are important in so many ways, not least because they connect us to the land, and this applies no matter where we live. Birdsong is as sweet in the city as in the countryside, and the cry of foxes at night is just as eerie. We are part of nature, and our voices communicate our needs, just like those of other animals. Our babies are born with one main way to let us know what they need – their voices. When we walk down a street, or stroll through a forest, the sounds of nature tell us so many things if we only listen. A sudden increase or decrease in natural sound makes us aware of danger, the night chorus of crows lets us know that the evening is upon us. Even without the slightest understanding of frequencies and ultrasound, we have proof all around us of the power of sound.

And do not despise the simplest sounds. One of my favourite noises is the gurgle of my coffee maker with its promise of sweet caffeine. There is powerful magic in simple, everyday things.

## The Harmonic Series and Natural Sound

Simply put, all music and the very concept of music itself, is derived from nature As Japanese composer, Toru Takemitsu said, *"Music should be based on a profound relationship to nature."*

The Harmonic Series is the chord of partials that vibrate when a natural tone is played. Its structure is unvarying, a mathematical harmonic series. The overtones usually sound as a single note (because they all vibrate as a chord at the same time). This overtone series is not only the basis of music but also speech, song, the ability to locate a sound, and the ability to distinguish between sounds. It's a natural physical phenomenon – the sounds within one sound, the sounds that combine to make a recognizable sound that we label as a note.

The harmonics are affected by many factors, including the material used to construct an instrument, and this creates different tonal qualities, or timbre. A middle C played on a piano, a violin, a xylophone or sung, can all be classed as the same note, but have different tonal qualities.

Pitch itself can be viewed as rhythm, because the rhythm or frequency of a note is defined as the number of occurrences of a repeating event, per unit of time. Manipulation of frequency alters pitch, and the Harmonic series therefore gives us the three foundations of music – timbre, pitch, and rhythm. What differs within each culture and era is the decision as to what constitutes a pleasing sound, or a discordant one.

These observations are offered as an overview and as such, are extremely simplified, and if you are interested in the subject, further study is highly recommended.

## Music, Religion and Culture

As music evolved in every culture, change could be seen as revolutionary. Sounds became attached to religious and societal symbolism, with some evolving into sacred, religious expression and some becoming taboo or devolving only on to certain groups.

Historically, women in particular were silenced and indeed, continue to be. In medieval times, the strictures on women were extreme. Laws across Europe punished them for "gossiping," and "scolding" which was an effective way to prevent the spread of information and limit the ways in which women could express discontent and expose ill-treatment. Gossip in this context was not idle chatter but the way in which women exercised power in a domestic and social setting, especially the wives and daughters of farmers, artisans and nobility.[10] Reputation across Europe, including Ireland, could determine your professional and social status, your credibility as a witness and your value as an ally. In many ways, overt and covert, women were excluded and silenced.

Religion had a huge influence on communication, music and society. Sacred music had to be kept distinct from, and uncontaminated by, secular music. There are endless examples across history, from Pope John banning the Major Third interval to current arguments about pop music at weddings or funerals. When both thoughts and emotions can be challenged by music, music is power. When music challenges the established order, it becomes subversive.

Music was overtly seen as magical in Ireland from early times, and we developed a rich and complex view that placed music at the heart of magic. But this was not exclusive to us by any means – in medieval Europe, music was seen as magical, because it was capable of revealing a system of sympathy and connection between this reality and underlying, hidden realities. The soul and the divine were presented as "perfectly harmonious." A supernatural healing of self was involved when listening to the right type of music, music that aligned us once more with that perfection. Hence the importance of perfect chords, and chord progressions.

At first, we may view the effect of sound on the listener as accidental but from very early times, humans learned that they could use sound to deliberately produce an effect, consistently and almost universally.

Society has always acknowledged the effect of music, especially on the young and impressionable. Attempts to ban or regulate certain types of music persist today as it did in the past – my personal favourite historical example being the many, many attempts by the British to regulate Irish music. American readers might reference the furore over Rock and Roll in the 1950s. When I was young, concerned parents in Ireland tried to have stickers placed on records that contained unsuitable lyrics (it only made us more determined to purchase them. Like, thanks for identifying the good stuff for us).

One interesting aspect of the ability of music to affect us is that you can produce cognitive dissonance between music and lyrics – the sweet sounds of *She Moves Through The Fair*, makes it a favourite song at Irish weddings but many forget that it is in fact a tragic tale of doomed love and early demise! In music theory, the field of Music Signification examines our complex associations and reactions to music.

All music evolves over time, and the type of music in fashion often reflects the mores of the day. For example, the Romantic period replaced the Classical in western music, as composers sought to give expression to individual feelings, over the order and elegance prized by the Classical period. In Irish music, we see that our formal music adapted to the upheavals and destruction of the seventeenth century and survived in folk music and in rebel songs. Music reflects the mood of the public, as well as the emotion of the individual.

Many studies have been performed on the benefits of music for children, including the benefit of learning to play an instrument or performing with others. For both children and adults, singing with others is proven to release endorphins and improve mental health. For children, music can speak when language has failed them, which makes it an invaluable tool for helping children in trauma e.g. in refugee camps. Music establishes a two-way benefit, enabling expression of trauma and then healing the same. In more normal circumstances, the benefits are still very clear – children who are involved in music learning, and performing, experience better levels of happiness, mental health, and socialization than their peers.

When it comes to expressing national identity, music is perhaps the most valuable tool at the propagandist's disposal. How we view ourselves as a nation influences our choices of anthems, from the state or national anthem to our beliefs about what music is viewed as "authentic" folk music. More than that, by choosing the correct anthems, we manipulate how the nation views itself. The pride felt as the National Anthem is played is taken for granted, but in Ireland we still recall the days when such a simple expression of identity was denied to us.

All this to say – Music shapes us, and we can shape ourselves through it, both as people and as communities.

## Silence

An often-overlooked part of sound, magic, and how it affects us, is silence. Silence is not merely the absence of noise, it is, among many other things, rhythm (think of staccato and syncopation,) as well as emphasis (making a phrase or passage stand out,) and it creates the moment of emotional crescendo, by forcing a pause.

In everyday life, silence is rare. Even what passes for silence isn't truly silent – and we become oblivious to the fact. I'm not just talking about the constant background hum of modern, technology laden, human existence but in nature herself, there is rarely silence. Something rustles, wind sighs, animals scurry. There was certainly far more "quiet" in our ancestors' lives. But true silence is creepy and unsettling. If you are at home among the relative quiet of the countryside, you may think you know what actual silence is but if every tiny noise was to suddenly cease, the hair on the back of your neck would rise.

I remember waking up once in the middle of the night, in a panic, unable to put my finger on what exactly had disturbed me. There had been a power cut while I slept, and all the electrical items that were on in the background turned off. The streetlights were gone, adding to the effect of heavy, oppressive silence. Whereas it might normally be an unusual sound that wakes one in the night, this time it was the absence of usual sound.

Silence can be a powerful weapon, as anyone who has dated a passive aggressive partner knows. Ostracizing someone by refusing to talk to them is a powerful statement, and from childhood onward we know that "I'm not speaking to you!" conveys our deepest chagrin. Nowadays we talk of ghosting, which is just a more elaborate way of not speaking to someone you no longer like. Being on speaking terms denotes a détente in any conflict. A familiar story in Ireland is the neighbour or family member at a funeral who admits, "We haven't spoken in years," over some small feud.

When we are deprived of autonomy, we speak of "having no voice," and "being silenced." Having our voice, our language, recognized and heard is a mark of status, privilege, and freedom. We see politically and culturally the effect of diminishing the voice of any community; from the oppression of the Irish language by Britain, to the way minority groups find themselves spoken over by more privileged communities. Women are particularly exposed to the practice of reduction and silencing. Studies show that when men are asked to quantify their contribution to a conversation versus that of the women present, they routinely underestimate how much time they were given to talk and overstate how much time a woman took up in the conversation. A woman who speaks one third as much as men do, is accused of hogging the conversation.

Add issues of race and socioeconomic status and it becomes clear that one of the mainstays of privilege is being heard and being listened to – and how we express ourselves is received differently depending on your gender and race. Women in general are accused by men of being over-emotional even when they respond calmly; Black women are accused of aggression for the same response.

To silence someone, or to misrepresent their message, inflicts real damage on individuals and communities; it has physical, mental and emotional repercussions.

Voice coach and therapist Jennifer Hamady reported her observations that while training singers:

> *"the majority of vocal issues people were dealing with had an emotional component. Even the most seemingly technical challenges—throat tension, trouble with certain notes or ranges, breathing—were almost always caused or exacerbated by personal issues."*

Silence is complicity, when it comes to issues of public justice. If you remain silent when others are speaking up, you are helping the oppressor. Neutrality can seem like a morally superior choice but silence in the face of injustice is just prioritizing your comfort. What we choose to be silent about reveals much about our true character and our moral compass.

Silent vigils and silent protests have become part of our political and social language for a reason. A crowd chanting slogans and making noise is undoubtedly powerful, but when the issue is solemn, or tragic, silence provokes a response that is reverent. It demands that people also be quiet and listen. Silence allows the issue to speak for itself, and when the silence is finally broken by a speech, that speech takes on a deeper significance because it was framed by silence.

Communities that have traditionally been ignored and silenced start to heal when their concerns are reported and debated. Individuals reflect the same – within family dynamics and the workplace, as well as socially among peers, an individual can find that their self-esteem and confidence improves when they are listened to with respect.

Silence is also comforting. When two people sit together and relax without the need for small talk, we call it "companionable silence." When terrible things happen, sometimes any comment we could make seems trite and useless – silence, simply showing up and being present, can be far better than words at times. In music terminology, a silence is called "a rest," and we might do well to think in terms of taking a rest, from noise in our personal lives.

Silence is also devotional, used to create spaces in which the sacred can be heard, or felt. Interestingly the most traditional way to mark this spiritual space is to border it with sacred words and music, letting the silence sit at its heart. In art people take about drawing negative space, the absence of mark making on a page. Similarly, in Draíocht Ceoil, we acknowledge the emphasis and magic that silence contributes to our workings with sound energy.

## Music and Memory

One of the reasons we instinctively see music as transcending the mundane is that music can connect us to a place, time or society, or individual, despite physical distance or the passing of years. It accesses parts of the brain that control memory. This has been established in recent studies thanks to increased research into Alzheimer's and dementia. One of the most promising areas of treatment for dementia is music therapy, designed to help stimulate the memory and calm the spirits of patients.

The late Dr. Oliver Sacks wrote[11] that he'd seen such patients shiver or weep while listening to music, leading to the realization that there is still a "self" within the patient, that only music can reach.

Jeff Anderson, M.D.[12] agrees, saying that music is like an anchor, grounding the patient in reality. According to research, music activates pasts of the brain untouched by the ravages of

Alzheimer's, improves mood, lifts depression. Research has demonstrated that music helps both caregivers and dementia patients, relieving feelings of depression and isolation in both. Again, music also helped recall a sense of self in dementia sufferers.

My father had vascular dementia and then Alzheimer's during the last ten years of life, and long after his memory disintegrated, music could trigger recall. It also soothed and calmed him. In social settings, he was increasingly isolated and going deaf exacerbated the issue – but whenever we had music, the Irish "singsong," he would perk up and show interest. During that period, although he lived with me and saw me every day as his primary caregiver, he was usually convinced I was the tea lady. However, at a New Year's Eve family gathering, I was asked to sing, and when I did so, he suddenly sat forward, eyes fixed on me, foot tapping and hand waving like a conductor. No praise was sweeter than his interest and enjoyment. For one moment, he crossed back into our world and communicated, through music.

Doctors and scientists are now confirming what caregivers in both family and nursing home situations already knew – music can bridge the gap, albeit briefly, between dementia sufferers and the world around them.

Sound operates as a time travel device, as well as allowing us to return to the same space, any space, and make fresh discoveries. Everyone will have individual sounds that affect them a little differently than most people – delve into that and try to untangle the reasons behind it. As a misophone, I have endless lists of sounds that I hate (or love) excessively but one sound, that of birdsong, consistently makes me happy in a bittersweet way. I cannot hear it, especially a blackbird (in Irish, the *londubh*) singing, without being transported to my childhood. As I get older, that wave of nostalgia is almost painful.

We may take for granted the power of sound to bring back memories, but it is magical when you stop to consider it. Long buried emotions, and old associations, become crystal clear with the right trigger. As with other uses of music, this can be a powerful force to manipulate emotion and prompt action in others.

## Chapter 3

# The Origins of Draíocht Ceoil

Our journey starts in the distant past, in Old Irish society, and in what we know of its culture and beliefs. We can trace the origins of this tradition in Early Irish Literature, most of it recorded in early Medieval times but linguistically and stylistically, attributable to a much older age.

Music is an art form rooted in time and place, each iteration of it being a commentary by a particular culture, at a particular point in time. But within a culture, it evolves from era to era, retaining some elements and discarding others. When we add language into this, the same applies. The use of poetic language in Draíocht Ceoil in ancient times is not the same as our modern approach to language. But by looking at the roots of the modern folk practice, we can see the relationships that have endured.

There are three main types or "strains" of Draíocht Ceoil mentioned in Old Irish literature.

*Geantraí*, the music of happiness; sweetness
*Goltraí*, the music of sadness; grief, lamentation
*Suantraí*, the music of sleep and meditation

According to the Early Irish legal tract, the *Uraicecht Becc* (known in English as The Small Primer,) the master harpist is the highest musician, and the one with greatest legal status. His duties include the ability to play music to bring on tears (*Goltraí*), to bring on joy (*Geantraí*) and to bring on sleep (*Suantraí*).

In one of our ancient stories, the "*Táin Bó Fraích*"[13], the harpists of Fraoch are named after the three strains of music and were said to be named by the great harpist, Uaithne, (which in turn is the name of the Harp of the Dagda, the great god). The harpists are inextricably linked to the Otherworld, to the magical elements of music. This same tale gives us many other insights into music, musicians and their status among the courtiers and elite of the time. At one point, Ailill and Medb ask Fraoch to join them in battle with his wealth and trumpets or hosts and musicians. Later, to heal his wounds caused by Ailill's treachery, Fraoch is placed in a bath of blood, and the seven trumpeters of his entourage played a healing song so powerful, thirty of Medb's courtiers died upon hearing it.

The references to music as a tool of the Otherworld, as magic or the means to make magic work, are too numerous to mention but they include the following:

In *The Battle of Moytura,* all three are used by Dagda to retrieve the Harp Uaithne, rather than slaughter remnants of the army of his enemies. In "*Cearbhall Ó Dálaigh,*" a tale within the Ulster Cycle, Cearbhall the poet escapes with his beloved from her own betrothal party to another suitor by playing a harp and putting the assembly asleep (*Suantraí*).

In "*Tochmare Étaine,*" Étaine, in her incarnation as a fly, uses her wings to create *Geantraí* music to soothe Midir's pain. This is an interesting example as the discovery is portrayed as inadvertent – in her agitation she creates music by accident, rather than deliberately intending to do so. However, once she has healed Midir's pain, they travel together, and she plays this music intentionally. It is also interesting that her healing power, both of music and touch, is portrayed as a side effect of the curse.[14] This side effect elevates her from a regular member of the Tuatha de Danaan elite, to a supernatural entity, capable of reincarnation and rebirth, as well as her supernatural powers connected to music.

In *The Children of Lir,* Aoife's remorse allows her to alleviate her own terrible curse on the children by giving them a gift of music so sweet that it will comfort all who hear it. As with Étaine's story, the power of music to mitigate terrible circumstances is emphasized. The Children are entitled to sing any of the three strains, but actively choose *Geantraí*, happiness, to alleviate their father's pain. The goodness of their natures would be apparent to the audience of the story by this choice, and the ability to sing *Geantraí* gives purpose to their lives. By their singing, the Children remind the mortal population of their story, from generation to generation, which, of course, recalls the role of the *Filí* themselves, memorizing stories and genealogy. Modern folk music in turn encodes the history and aspirations of the people.

Other powers attributed to music in the Old Irish literature include healing, and the power over death itself. In the story of Donn Bó, although he was killed in the Battle of Allen, Bó's head retained the ability to sing after death, and his songs of *Suantraí* and *Goltraí* provoked such remorse in his enemies that they reattached his head and brought him back to life. He sang to fulfill a promise to Fergal, also slain in battle, that he would entertain him (sing for him) wherever he was that evening.

Each of the three strains of music could be used to heal or punish – e.g. Aillén and his *timpán* (a small stringed instrument) present mortal danger to Tara and the Tuatha de Danaan. In the tale *Fionn agus Aillén*, where the power to soothe asleep is used as a weapon, it is so powerful only deep magic, "poison magic," can undo it.

This continues into modern day folklore. Fairy music can lull unsuspecting mortals and place them in danger, and the capricious nature of the Sidhe is reflected in their response to musical talent among mortals. Some chants are held to be dangerous, to hex or ill-wish, while the very ability to play above the normal level of skill marks the player out as different, perhaps even the recipient of unnatural gifts from either the Devil or the Sí depending on your viewpoint.

### The Importance of Music to Early Irish Society

Early Irish texts provide evidence that there is a continuity of belief in magic and music, and the use of music as a conduit between the otherworldly and mundane, noting that it exists in both pre-Christian and Christian contexts.[15]

It is important to bear in mind two things when discussing music in both the ancient and the medieval period. The first is that the world was quieter. There were the sounds of human occupations, the sounds of nature, the sounds of livestock. The constant hum of traffic, of electricity, of industrial machinery didn't intrude into everyday life. Nor was music or entertainment available on demand. It couldn't be prerecorded, played on demand, or easily accessed. The instruments to provide it and the skill to perform it were valuable commodities.

Secondly, much of the actual music itself is lost to us or only survives in remnants and the further back we go, the truer this holds. What we *can* access from the existing literature is knowledge about how the Early Irish viewed music, its importance culturally and spiritually, and its relationship to magic or supernatural activity.

The literature also shows how music straddled both mundane activities – entertainment at gatherings and feasts, for example – and Otherworldly (i.e. not of this reality, supernatural) encounters – especially when Otherworld entities intrude upon or intersect with, mundane human activities. Music is portrayed in so many ways – at fairs, in the home, in monasteries, as prophecy, as performance, as a message from the Otherworld, all together.

Music is the oldest, and most instinctive, form of creative play known to man[16] Our ability to communicate through sound is inextricably intertwined with our evolution as humans, and our abilities to form community.

## Instruments in Ireland

That music formed part of ceremonies and rituals, we know both from literary and archaeological sources. The Prehistoric Horns of the National Museum of Archaeology are treasures that give us some sense of the importance and solemnity our ancestors may have experienced. The recordings of the horns in the twentieth century, eerie sounds that reverberate in your chest, yielded interesting ideas about the physicality needed to play them. For example, the same type of circular breathing needed to get sound from a didgeridoo works on the larger horns.[17]

Ancient instruments were varied and impressive, from the earliest attempts to create music outside of our own voice to the ornate Bronze Age horns now housed in the National Archaeology Museum, Dublin. Bone flutes were used, one of the earliest recorded in Europe being made from a swan's radius bone (found in the Geissenklosterle Cave, Germany). Similar bone flutes have been found in Irish sites, as have Elder-wood whistles. Stones with naturally occurring holes were used as bird lures, as well as possibly simple whistles or crude ocarinas.

Archery bows were used (and still are used in this manner in parts of Africa). One end is held in the mouth and the other end is on the ground – the string is plucked or struck to manipulate sound. Hollow sticks were used as clapsticks, much like the indigenous people of Australia use them today.

But without a doubt the most impressive of the ancient instruments are the large horns dating from 3,500 to 2.500 BCE – the Bronze Age. If in Dublin there are many reasons to visit the National Archaeology Museum, not least their impressive collection of ancient instruments. It took pioneering experimental work to decipher how they were played, to record them and to extrapolate their usage based on the range of notes and tones available, as well as the effort and skill needed to extract sound from them. Ritual use seems almost a given, their very appearance suggesting ceremonial power and status. The effort required to make them involves collaboration between different crafts – from metallurgy to design – suggesting their importance to the community. I strongly recommend listening to the recordings of the horns – available online on the "Ancient Music of Ireland" website.

Also, among the collections in the National museum are crotals, handbells and some round discs. We have no surviving tradition of how to use these discs, but theories include rattles or tiny cymbals.

The evolution of musical instruments in Ireland is tied to the way society itself developed. For example, the advent of agriculture brought hollow horned livestock such as cows to Ireland, and in turn, the creation of bone horns that could be blown. Perhaps the most important instrument to develop from the introduction of agriculture is the *Bodhrán*, the unique drum of Irish folk music. A *Bodhrán* is a fixed frame tambour drum, played by striking a stick (now usually wood, but often referred to as a bone, perhaps hinting at its original form). The tambour drum is common to many cultures but the way we play it, with the stick (cipín) is unique to Ireland. In my thirty years behind the counter of my family music shop, I explained the origins of the drum from a winnowing tool to a skinned instrument more times than I can possibly count. The reintroduction of the *Bodhrán* in the folk revival of the 1960s sometimes leads people to assume the *Bodhrán* is a relatively modern instrument, but it has a long and rich tradition in Ireland.

The word *Bodhrán* is generally held to derive from *bodhar*, a word associated with both deafness and sound, since early times. Like many Irish words, it has more than one meaning and association. It appears in the translation of the

Rosa Angelica (an English text) in the 16th century with an unambiguous meaning of drum. The importance of the drum in Irish music into modern times is illustrated in a nineteenth century painting entitled "Snap Apple Night" *(Daniel Maclise, circa 1833*) depicting a *Bodhrán* player along with fiddle, pipes and flute, entertaining locals who dance.

The *Bodhrán* is still an integral part of Irish music and has enjoyed a renewed popularity as an aid to meditation and journeying. The note of the instrument varies depending on its size and the depth of the rim, and the use of your non-striking hand to manipulate the skin adds a wide variety of tones, making it an ideal tool for Draíocht Ceoil. My personal recommendation is a 16" or 18" with deep rim, and to buy from an Irish maker. There is no substitute for an instrument made within the tradition of making here.

The violin or fiddle is another stalwart of Irish music, along with flutes, whistles and drums. In recent years guitars, banjos and bouzoukis have entered the scene, adding new dimensions to the tradition.

It is worth noting that there is a very strong tradition of classical music in Ireland, and alongside it, new forms of music from pop to rap still express the feelings and opinions of the population. Artists like Kneecap combine music and words with activism, and new additions to our cultural landscape include outstanding artists like Denise Chaila.

## Irish Music

Four scales (or modes) are commonly used in traditional Irish music – Ionian, Mixolydian, Dorian and Aeolian.

Dorian and Aeolian are both minor scales. Ionian is the most common Major, and Dorian the most common Minor scale used. These modes are what make Irish music so recognizable, the use of what in modern music are the D and G scales, and the use of mixed minor scales to create a uniquely Irish sound. Different cultures have their own unique music: while Draíocht Ceoil is an Irish tradition it is extremely adaptable to other cultures and is found in most cultures in some form or other.

## Draíocht Ceoil in Folklore

Irish folklore is filled with stories of Fairy music, always the sweetest and most lovely music heard, and the most dangerous. It can lead you astray, and any mortal with the nerve to try to play it is either punished for failing or…if they are talented enough to play it well…stolen away to play for the wee folk.

Fairy music has its origins in an early tale *The Chase of Slieve Fuad*, where not only does *Suantraí* occur but the victims are, crucially, led astray. It shows *Suantraí* as a weapon, the afflicted sinking to the ground in a deathlike trance. When the Fianna try to use their own sound magic, it is hijacked by the enemy and leads the Fianna themselves astray. The initial targets of this attack include the musician, Dara, someone whose presence is apparently vital to the success of the Fianna's hunt. Dara in turn uses a *timpán* to counteract the effect of the *Suantraí* and then the Fianna are only restored to health by drinking from a magical horn. At one point, fearing they were close to death, Fionn asks Dara "to play one of his sweet, sad tunes, that they might hear the music of his *timpán* before they died." Thus, the importance of music is reinforced. Dara's heroic effort to perform this last sweet song ultimately enables the Fianna to escape. Music is a strategic weapon, in the struggle against their enemy.

In modern times, music from the Otherworld – usually heard near Dúns, Raths and prehistoric remnants – is seen as alluring but ultimately dangerous. Musicians, as shown in the stories surrounding figures like Turlough O'Carolan, are seen as "touched" or indeed cursed by musical talent, or as having exchanged something valuable (sight, or mobility) in return for musical ability. We see this trope in many cultures still, even up to legendary Blues musicians meeting the devil at the crossroads or rock stars selling their souls to the devil.

We also see music used as an excuse; possession by music is blamed for all kinds of antics. Music is so powerful the person's autonomy or responsibility is diminished. The effect of music on a crowd is recorded in stories of weddings and funerals, gatherings and Fairs. The British were reportedly so afraid of the effect of music on the Irish – especially the *Bodhrán* and the pipes – that they were moved to outlaw it.

Since earliest times, music has been used as a weapon in Irish culture. To be a warrior in Old Ireland was to have a status second only to the Chieftain and to be a member of the elite. Stories of Na Fianna show that the warrior caste was also "outside the law," to some degree, enjoying privileges denied to others and an amount of social mobility. Whereas a lot of modern culture pits the idea of being a warrior in opposition to any creative or cultured pursuit, Old Ireland valued both physical and creative skill in a warrior. Warrior culture was inherently violent, and to our modern eyes, brutal – but it coexisted alongside a highly elevated status for musicians and poets. Warriors in particular were linked to music. In the story of Don Bó mentioned above, Donn Bó's head is chosen from a pile of the heads of slain warriors because it was singing, and such was the beauty of its *Goltraí*, Bó provoked shame in the enemy King and regret for the slaughter. In a symbolic act, the Chieftain reattaches Donn Bó's head and sends him off home. Music is presented in this story as a diplomatic and spiritual tool, restoring peace, prompting reparation. But music and verse were also displayed as battle magic, and as weapons in their own right.

In the story of *Fionn agus Aillen* also touched on above, Aillen is a powerful figure, who visits Tara at Samhain, and using his *timpán*, plays music to lull the court asleep (*Suantraí*) then sets fire to the place, using a blast of fire from his throat (perhaps in itself a reference to Draíocht Ceoil). The king offers the leadership – and more, the inheritance of – the Fianna (a legendary group of warriors, almost a kingship in its own right) to whomever defeats Aillen. Fionn accepts the challenge and is gifted a spear that can counteract Aillen's magical music. Music is clearly a magical weapon, only contestable by using another magical weapon. Having defeated Aillen, Fionn ceases his *timpán* and his flute as spoils. A *timpán* was considered on a par with a harp and an acceptable substitute for one.

Another instance where music itself threatens the position of authority is the story of *Labhraí Loingseach,* a tale that every schoolchild in Ireland is told at some point. Labhraí had a secret, which threatened his entire position as a king. In ancient Irish culture, a king had to be physically perfect and poor Labhraí was far from this – he had donkeys ears hidden under his head of hair. Every time he had to have his hair cut, he killed the barber to preserve his secret – until one young man was chosen and his mother begged that he be spared. No one knew why the King murdered the unfortunate hairdressers, only assuming he was under some kind of geas – a magical obligation – to do so. The King promised to spare the young man, if he promised to keep the secret. This worked for a while, but the burden of knowing something so terribly dangerous, and of keeping a secret that went against all the standards of kingship, nearly drove the poor boy mad. On the advice of a Druid, he went to the forest and told his secret to an oak tree and unburdened his mind. But when the court musician went to make a new harp, he cut a branch from that very oak tree to make it. The new harp sang *Firenne,* truth, and it's first act was to sing out "Labhraí Loingseach has donkey ears!" In the children's story, the king realized that no one minded about his donkey ears and thus he never had to kill a barber again.

This is actually tale adapted from *King Gyeongmun's Ear,* a Korean folktale from the 9th century, but in the Irish version, a harp plays the crucial role of outing the King's private shame. It can be assumed that the original Irish version probably ended with the removal of the king's power. Variations can be found in the National Folklore Collection[18] and in them the king sometimes sails away or leaves in shame, never to be seen again.

In its most popular form, the tale reflects the importance of music politically, and socially, attributes magical power to sound and echoes the power of the *Filí* to raise a blemish on the cheek of a dishonest or dishonorable king, thus removing him from power.

## Music in Irish Society

Musicians are accorded a lot of respect from early times to present day, especially in Irish culture. Throughout history they have taken on the role of expressing the feelings of the population at both a local and national level. From rebel ballads to modern performers and activists like Kneecap, they voice both consent and dissent. The *Aos Dana* (people of skill) were the caste that included poets, doctors, Brehons (lawyers) and within the designation of *File* (poet) certain musicians – especially harpists – whose skills were considered to be otherworldly. This special position in society survived well into early modern Ireland – indeed, to some degree still survives. Brehon Law was clear on the importance and protection accorded to Musicians.

Musical forms evolve and survive as time passes. To give just one example – from the battle Rosc of Early Irish society, we see the *laoi filíocht* (patriotic verse, set to music) of medieval Ireland, and finally the popular rebel songs of modern Ireland. Each in their own era represented the attitudes of the people and the accepted public order but as the very concept of Irishness came under increasing attack from Britain, they began to represent the aspirations of the nation.

As we move into early modern Ireland, the impact of colonial violence on society sees the old order overturned. The

Chieftains – even those who had taken the knee to Elizabeth and received titles in return – were in disarray, either dispossessed or fled, and with it the system that upheld and protected the Poetic schools. The *Filí* order was irreparably damaged. But like much of Irish culture, it was kept alive by the people, in the folk music, the songs, the storytelling, and folklore. Similarly, the more esoteric aspects, the belief in the Otherworld and the skill in invoking it, the magical elements, were preserved by the people.

When we look at folklore, and folk magic, there are clear echoes of the past. The use of Laments, Keening, modern versions of Rosc, Aisling (prophetic or dream poetry) and *laoi filíocht* all reflect earlier beliefs and practices. More than this, they encode them and preserve them – albeit in a more fragmented form – for use by the populace. Where once a File stood as the arbiter of disputes, the repository of local knowledge and lore, these roles also fragmented. Never again would the poet wield so much power – but in their place, we see people held to have "the cure" for various conditions (afflicting both human and livestock) and those held to have the sight, the power of divination. There are those whose role it was to keen. Perhaps the figure most closely representing the old order is the *Bean Feasa* – the woman of knowledge, who appear throughout folklore and stories as the negotiator between the Otherworld and the people, as the holder of knowledge (medicinal and magical) and the arbiter of disputes. She often stands for local native ability against the formal, perhaps foreign, influence of the Doctor or Priest.

The *Bean Feasa* understands the use of Draíocht Ceoil, from the humming of bees to creating charms and spells, from the power of words to the dangers of fairy music. But they were by no means the only ones in the community to use Draíocht Ceoil – more than perhaps any type of folk magic, it became an integral part of daily life, or indeed, perhaps it always was. The humble activities of the plebs rarely make it into the lofty tomes of history, and Irish Sagas are no exception to this rule. At any rate, the ways in which it permeates life in Ireland are innumerable – lullabies to protect children, chants to help churn the milk, songs to bake bread, old stories and knowledge sung over the hearth, or at communal gatherings and chanting (extemporaneous chanting) while spinning are just a few examples. People, of course, sang and made music for pleasure, but they also combined this with an attempt to imbue a task with good luck, or using a repetitive task to daydream a desire into being.

An example of the latter would be songs and music used while sowing, or harvesting, crops. These obviously helped pass the time – my father spent many summers in the 1930s and 1940s in Wicklow on his cousin's farm, as a child, helping with both tasks. The days were broken up and made easier by singing, sometimes men singing to women and vice versa or perhaps competitions between rival groups vying to be the best singers or compose the funniest verses. But between these bursts of creativity, there were songs about a good harvest, a good spring, the need for good weather and so on. This reminded the workers of the ultimate goal and many of the songs were about love of the land, the beauty of the land, the land as a beautiful woman. This reinforced the connection, patriotic and spiritual, to the land itself.

An example of the former is the habit of women while spinning (or indeed, doing any repetitive task) to sing and hum and burst into extemporaneous verse. Sometimes these sounded like nonsense songs, sounds and musical phrases that have no translation into spoken language, but the notes and the pitch evoke a reaction in both the singer and the listener.

## Fairy Music

Folklore abounds with stories of Otherworldly musicians, or the Otherworld reaching out to mortal musicians, making the musician themselves a person who can attract the attention of the Sí, hear the unearthly strains of fairy music and by extension move between the two realities.

The National Folklore collection has many stories of ordinary people hearing fairy music and being led astray, a tradition that owes its origins directly to much older talesAgain, in *The Chase of Slieve Fuad,* when *Suantraí* occurs the victims are not merely lulled to sleep, butweakened and confused. When they in turn use their own sound magic, it is hijacked by the enemy and leads even the Fianna themselves astray. This filters down into songs like *Amhrán na Síogaí* (Song of the Fairies) with its story of a man who is fairy-led, ending up in the Hall of Fionnbheara, (a King of the Sí) under the mountain known as Cnoc Meá – ending with a warning to others to avoid the area and not follow fairy music.

This interference from the Otherworld, conveyed using music and sound, is the origins of the fairy pipers, the siren-like singing of the fairy woman, and tales of individuals being led into danger if they follow supernatural music, especially at night, around raths and Dúns.

In collections of folk music compiled over the last few centuries, there are many pieces whose composition is attributed directly or indirectly to the Sidhe. In Donegal, the tune *A Fairy Reel* was reportedly heard on the road home by a well-known local fiddle player. John Mhosaí, in the mid nineteenth century. He heard fairy music, listened and memorized it and upon returning to his home, started to play the piece. He never claimed to have composed it, only to have lifted it whole from the fairy folk. As musicians were held in high esteem by the Sidhe, it seems they sometimes "gifted" one of their own pieces to a player.

The Sidhe were not above abducting musicians or luring them away, The National Folklore Collection being full of such tales. This one in particular gives a sense of the ecstatic effect of music on the receptive musician:

*"So beautiful it was that the fiddler was visibly moved and thrown into an ecstasy. His eyes shone like brilliant stars. His body trembled while his hands clenched tightly his beloved fiddle. All the company looked on and appeared to be greatly frightened at the appearance of their beloved fiddler. Not a word did he utter, but listened with rapt attention as the music drew nearer and sounded sweeter. All believed that it could not be produced by any mortal person. No one but the fairies could bring out such delightful notes on a violin. Suddenly the fiddler arose, his face all aglow. He rushed to the door and out into the open. All voices could be heard calling on the fiddler to stop. But still the music continued although it grew fainter and fainter ...The fiddler followed the fairy music."*[19]

The other common story is of a musician finding inspiration in liminal spaces, especially in the local archaeological and natural features that are associated with the good neighbours. It was considered unlucky to linger at places like duns and cairns especially at night: but some courted this interaction with the Otherworld. Turlough O'Carolan was said to sleep in these places, to receive *Imbas* (inspiration) and at least one piece, *Bridget Cruise*, was composed as a result (recounted by the collector Francis O'Neill). The fiddler, Mickey "Simey" Doherty, was recorded in 1949 playing *A Jig Learnt from the Fairies*, a slip jig that was taught to a local man by the fairies, handed down to Mickey Doherty's uncle and then on to Mickey himself.

Within the same collection of recordings are stories of fiddlers whose meager repertoires were magically enhanced by a friendly, otherworldly stranger or by entertaining fairy hosts. The great Coleman brothers from Sligo, whose talent straddled both sides of the Atlantic, were held to have had their prowess bestowed on them by the fairies, a tale handed down to locals including the Sligo fiddle player Fred Finn, who told it to historian P.J. Duffy, who in turn retold to RTE's Harry Bradshaw.[20] It worth noting that the Colemans lived in early twentieth century, not the eighteenth or nineteenth. These are living traditions.

These old songs and tunes are accompanied by the tales of their origins, and this is invaluable. On their own, divorced from this context, we would be left with tantalizing hints in the titles or lyrics, but thanks to the foresight of the Folklore Commission in the early twentieth century, we have the history of the music, its local significance, its ties to the landscape and to mythology and a record of beliefs.

Some are stories of magical revenge (e.g. *The Bruckless Drowning*) some of monsters who live among us, such as "Petticoat Loose" and many of interactions with the Good Neighbours. Stories of the *Bean Sidhe* (Banshee) and warnings of death, or at the other extreme, of mortal women entering the hidden world of the Sidhe under the hills to act as a kind of midwife to a pregnant fairy woman (*Amhrán an Frág* is one song tied to such a legend, and it also warns of the danger of making a wish, without thinking it through. You simply never know who might be listening in the Irish landscape).

Tunes such as *The Lone Bush* were tied to warnings about interfering with fairy trees, something no sensible farmer or labourer in Ireland would ever do. Immediate calamity would follow – in my own family, one such story persists of an inconveniently situated fairy tree on family property that in the nineteen seventies was blamed for an accident, after the unfortunate victim tried to cut a branch from it.

Ordinary folk also reported hearing fairy music, near raths.[21]

> *"About thirty years ago or maybe more music was heard in Ballaghanea. It was first heard at rocks in the river which flows along the Mullagh road. It was then heard crossing a hill called*

> *the Round Hill. It then visits all the forts in Ballaghanea and then ceases to be heard. It sounded sometimes like the music of a tin whistle and at other times it sounds like a flute. It was so sweet that it would lift the heaviest heart."*

Or often on the way home late at night.[22]

> *"One time a man was going home from his ceilidh. It would be between 11 and 12 o clock in the night. He was going by a fort and he suddenly heard lovely music, it was the music of a fiddle. He stopped and immediately the music stopped. He moved on and the music started again. Then he heard the fairies laughing. The wisest among us ignored the music, and hurried home. Some brave (or foolhardy) souls followed the music or entered the spaces where it was heard."*

An intriguing tale from Galway has a man enter a house where he heard music. The people there offered him food and drink, which he refused (a common theme in encounters with the Good Neighbours is never to accept food or drink from them) hinting that he realized the supernatural nature of the gathering. He then sees his aunt, whom he knew to be dead, and makes his escape. Later he behaves in a way as to suggest madness, and the priest confines him to his house and recommends emigration.[23]

Fairy music did not only include singing and instruments. Fairy women often appeared while humming to themselves. Folk music was often transmitted and committed to memory by humming, including fairy tunes, and in folklore, humming could summon fairies or open liminal spaces. There were some remedies available to those caught in Fairy magic. Fairy music that was designed to lure mortals could be counteracted by turning your jacket, or turning your coat inside out to break the spell.

One story that manages to combine several of these elements is that of William Reynolds[24]. A "stray sod" is the belief that a sod of earth in an otherwise normal field was enchanted or fairly touched and would lead you into the hands of the fairies. The Sidhe were seen as capricious, dangerous, and mischievous and these stray sods were typical of their pranks. William Reynolds was humming as he crossed the field, thus opening himself to the power of the Good Neighbours. He stepped on a stray sod and fell foul of the Sidhe until he broke the charm by turning his jacket inside out.

As late as the nineteen thirties, people considered the presence of fairies at sacred wells and old sites as completely normal. Stories in the National Folklore collection are not all of times gone by – many refer to recent events, for example, the story from Kilmorgan[25] of fairies singing a well-known tune by a sacred well, the previous May Eve (1930s).

There is no room in this book for an exhaustive exploration of the way Irish music and stories were connected and used to convey our folklore and beliefs but I hope this has given you some sense of the rich and varied heritage encoded in our music and stories – and of the relationship between music and magic. The importance of the connection between the lore and the music cannot be overstated – in a society suffering upheaval and disaster under occupation, this holistic tradition kept our magical beliefs and practices alive.

## Otherworldly Musicians

In a society that prized musicians, it is not surprising to find many of them appearing time and again from the old literature to modern folklore. These stories tell us much about the magical power of music throughout Irish history.

Cascorach is a famous otherworldly personage appearing in texts such as *Accalam na Senorach* (The Colloquy with Ancient Men) where we are told he "took his *timpán,* tuned it, and on it played a volume of melody the equal of which for sweetness … the clergy had never heard. Upon them fell a fit of slumber and of sleep" (*Suantraí*).

The supernatural player Senbec, a "wee man" performs for Cuchulainn, in the *tale Comrac Con Chulainn*. This story illustrates all three strains of magical music, played in succession causing Cuchulainn to cry, laugh and sleep in turn.

There are many more, from another "wee man" Cnu Derail, to the nine pipers of Sid Breg, and not to omit the musical prowess of entities such as Lugh, Dagda, Midir, *Bríd*. The tradition of keening at wakes (*Caoin*ean) is directly descended from the lament of Brigid on the death of her son. Keening is one of the most famous examples of magical, and supernatural, use of music (more on this later).

The early Christian Church in Ireland enjoyed a syncretic relationship with the Pagan past, both acknowledging the reality of the Otherworld and simultaneously attempting to sanitize it – but crucially, despite some modern misconceptions, it rarely sought to destroy it. St Patrick himself comments on Cascorach's music, acknowledging its supremacy and beauty. He admits the "twang of the fairy spell that infests it," but he merely warns against becoming addicted to it.

The *Filí* retained their favoured place in society, and much of their political influence and power throughout Christian Ireland. The Harpists also retained their place, and added to the ranks of musicians were the clergy and sacred music. The Christian church added their own take on supernatural music, from angelic music without any visible performer to tracts detailing the sacred music of the heavens. They added their own rich imagery and beliefs to the body of magical reasoning regarding music and the power of sound, describing Heaven as inherently musical, and accepting the power of music and words in this reality.

## Modern Irish Folk Music

To outside ears Irish music and other folk music can be surprising, i.e. not ending on the expected note and not conforming to the classical progressions with which they are familiar. As the great Thomas Moore said, "Even in their liveliest strains, we find some melancholy note intrude – some minor third or flat seventh- which throws its shade as it passes and makes even mirth interesting" (Thomas More, writing to Stevenson, 1807).

Irish music as a whole, ends on one of four notes, Doh Ray So or La. Most is written in the key of D or G – hence the importance of the D whistle or flute.

Folk music is sometimes defined as anonymous pieces, "music of the folk" rather than of a known writer or composer. A key element is that it is reshaped by the "folk" over generations. This is a useful definition when talking about the history of folk music, but I prefer the wider definition in Irish of *'Amhráin atá I mbéal an phobail'* – songs that are in the mouth of the people, which includes music that is current as well as traditional. Musicians like Padraig Jacks, an Irish-speaking musician from the Aran islands, are creating wonderful Irish folk music that we cannot exclude from definitions of the same. Both definitions are correct in that the songs of the people change over time – pop music, Irish hip hop, Irish rap artists, music created by Irish artists with a different ethnic and cultural background, all in turn becomes 'songs in the mouth of the people.'

The type of music each culture views as their own affects how they use sound in magic. In Irish traditions, the three strains *of Geantraí, Goltraí* and *Suantraí* are found equally in Irish folk music and folk magic, to the present day. But we as modern people harness the new sounds and technologies to create. Irish Rap has an unmistakably "Irish" sound – Denise Chaile's track *Anseo* being a perfect example. The Xi'an Sí, a group of classical Chinese musicians from Xi'an, China, used traditional Classical Chinese instruments to play famous Irish pieces.

The brought a stately, measured tempo that actually returned work like O'Carolan's *Air* to its original form, while played on instruments far removed from the Irish tradition. Similarly, when composing a working for magical purposes we can draw on every type of music, anything that we are inspired to write or that has meaning for us whether a pop song, a traditional ballad or a classical sonata. What remains consistent is the need to observe the three strains, and to choose accordingly.

### *Exercise*

I would recommend listening to music at random, e.g. radio or Spotify play lists, and ask yourself which of the strains each invokes. Look for "fight music" and "heartbreak music," as well as happy, dance tunes. Listen also to traditional Irish music, of any type (Ballads, Session Music, Classical Irish) and see if you can make a link between them and a modern Pop/Rock/ Rap or whatever equivalent. Drawing links between music is an important part of opening yourself to the effect of music, and sound. Teach your brain to think in terms of the three strains, and how they affect you and others.

Where possible sing out loud and dance around. Not so much that it will make you any more magical, but it will certainly improve your mood.

## Chapter 4

# Sound in Draíocht Ceoil

In Draíocht Ceoil, certain sounds are held to have specific power. This is equally true of music, non-lexical sounds and words, although it also applies to natural and incidental sounds. All sound has a role to play in constructing a spell but music, poetry and the use of nonsense words and lilting, are the most potent.

We will look at the inherent power of words in a further chapter, so for now let's concentrate on sound itself. Creating a spell in Draíocht Ceoil is a layered process, and words are really the final layer, so at first, we will concentrate on sound, and sound as a channel to magical energy.

Music can be defined as "organized sound," and notes can be both powerful in themselves, and also gain power because of their relation to the sounds preceding and following them.

Music gains importance through association. Some music is instantly recognizable as belonging to a particular culture or region. The association of a certain type of sound with a national identity that further roots that power in a magical tradition. It also gains power through emotional and intellectual connections e.g. the power to evoke and manipulate emotion, or to awaken national or tribal associations.

In Irish musical traditions, we see the imitation of sounds of nature that trigger human emotions and memories. For example, vocal and instrumental sound mimicking birdsong, thunder, or waves. Any sound that mimics a sound found in nature has *Brí* energy (energy of wild places). This is found in both the mundane and magical musical traditions.

Modern Irish music has embraced modern technology with modern artists such as Denise Chaila, KneeCap and RíRá pushing the definition of Irish musical identity. The use of electronics in music is a facet of the modern era, but that doesn't mean we can't embrace electronic sounds in Draíocht Ceoil. In fact, I have a fascination with what I call e-witchcraft in general, using a modern medium to deliver magic. In Draíocht Ceoil, technology provides a way to harness sounds that would otherwise be hard to source.

As mechanical and electronic sounds have *Bua* energy, they can fit in very well into crowd magic, urban energy and so on. Both *Brí* and *Bua* sound energy can be used in magic.

That being said, some of the oldest expressions of music and sound remain the foundation for Draíocht Ceoil today. Not only are they the fundamentals of music itself, but they also each have an effect on the individual and on this physical reality.

In this section, let's look at the most common forms of making "organized sound" and their affect upon us.

## Chanting

I have included Chanting here, rather than in Chapter 7 Words and Draíocht Ceoil, because it has the same effect whether using words or solely music.

In the early nineteen sixties, chanting (with or without words) was found to "charge" the brain – something perhaps instinctively understood by early people. Certainly chants – including extemporaneous chanting, chanting composed on the spot – have been an intrinsic part of Draíocht Ceoil since the heyday of the *Filí* class. Both the rhythm and tones of the chant have distinct power over our emotions and intellect. Chanting has also been found to increase concentration and to have positive effects on mindfulness – to increase the awareness of one's present condition and aid detachment and objectivity. The repetitive chanting of mantras in one tradition or the extemporaneous chanting of another have the same practical effects and you will find traditions of chanting in both spiritual and secular practices worldwide. When linked to spiritual practices we tend to call them mantras or prayers, but whatever the label the effects are the same.

Mindfulness through chanting has become an important tool for treatment of depression and anxiety, and for helping magical practitioners to focus, an integral part of spell casting in every tradition. It can also increase objective emotional response, which lessens the dangers posed by subjective or reactive, emotional responses. Magical workings can be emotionally charged but should never be knee-jerk reactions.

Chanting is used in many cultures to commune with ancestors, to prevent illness, to enhance spiritual practices and to facilitate sacred ceremonies. In Draíocht Ceoil it is also used to attune the mind to magical energy, to charge and amplify that energy and to aim it.

Chanting can also be a solitary practice or a communal one, and both have different effects or the same effects to differing degrees. Whether sacred or magical or mundane, the common thread is that it involves focused intentional action i.e. an emphasis on an intentional outcome as the focus of the chanting. The chant itself in Draíocht Ceoil is the mechanism of this focus and intention – the words or sounds chosen carry the intent.

Draíocht Ceoil is not alone in ascribing particular associations with sound – similar beliefs are observed in Hindi and Buddhist chants, where mantras are associated with particular deities, or expressions of belief. In the Irish folk magic tradition, however, these associations are less sacred than magical and reflect a belief in the ever-present magical energy. Individuals are, of course, welcome to ascribe sacred meaning in their own practice but as a folk practice, the belief lies in magical not spiritual action.

## Humming

Humming is one of the most useful practices in Draíocht Ceoil, allowing you to modulate pitch and tone and imitate instrumental sound. It has a long association with magic as demonstrated in the National Folklore Collection. Ghosts and other supernatural entities manifest by humming tunes, much as the fairy musicians show themselves to unwary mortals by playing music.[26] In everyday domestic life, humming while spinning, milking cows or churning butter was held to make the task easier and smoother, and to soothe animals.

Even more intriguing are stories where humming actually summons fairies. In the story *of John Joyce of Ballyroughan*, the unfortunate Joyce was carrying a saddle on his back one night and humming a tune as he went, only to find a fairy catching a ride on the saddle. She danced on his hat to the tune of the music, and when he reached home, she asked him what he was planning with the saddle. He had borrowed it to bring a horse to market, so she wished him "the best of luck" which ensured he sold the horse for a great price the next day. Humming was seen as a way to open the liminal spaces between worlds, especially around "long hollows" (earthworks) and the forts (duns and raths) and the transmission of otherworldly music to mortal players was often done through the medium of humming.[27] Fairy women in particular appear to men, humming away to themselves, in many recorded stories.[28]

In Draíocht Ceoil we use humming in many circumstances, from impromptu workings or as a way to create a safe space in public, to planned and complex workings. It is an instrument, accessible to most and free to use, with the added benefit of being a very traditional practice.

Another interesting use of humming is to avoid breaking a taboo or *geas* of silence or to avoid losing a bet of the same. Folklore has variations on a similar theme: a couple argue over who should do a particular task, and vow that the first to speak loses and must do the chore. The woman is spinning, or churning, the man carving or cobbling. A third party arrives and asks a question, to which the woman replies by humming, the man speaks and loses the bet. Sometimes they both continue to hum, and the unfortunate visitor retires in confusion. In one story, however, a British officer threatens the couple with a revolver, and the woman speaks, thus losing the bet.[29] Here we see the use of humming as a specific way to communicate without words, a way to navigate an exchange without breaking a taboo.

Widows and their daughters are a recurring motif in the Irish folklore collection, worth noting. Widows had a special status in society, both revered and feared in different ways and there seems to be a special store placed in their daughters, perhaps as seemingly unprotected females, or women in special need of good luck. They certainly seem to have more than their fair share of otherworldly encounters. In *The Widow's Daughters* we see humming performed as *Suantraí*, lulling a hag to sleep so the young girl can steal her coins.[30] We know that the old tunes were preserved in communities by women who learned to hum them, so they could be passed down to a new generation. The magical strains of music were likewise encoded, in stories of fairy folk, ghosts and mysterious entities humming *Suantraí*, *Goltraí* and *Geantraí*.

A similar range of effects can be found in Lilting, the traditional Irish music vocal practice of singing traditional tunes, using nonsense words, to create a rhythmic melody.

## Hissing

Closely allied to humming, is "hissing." This is generally associated with malignant intent, although there are examples of it being used in healing (to scare away the disease). Hissing is a low sibilant noise formed by pushing air through the teeth or tongue (hissh or hissss) and has elements common to both high and low pitch sounds. It therefore combines "good" and "bad" energy to create something truly *Breacc* (Speckled, mixed). It is not a commonly used technique – there are few situations calling for it – but, when necessary, it is a powerful sound.

Hissing has several deep associations that add to its importance as a magical sound. One obvious one is the way a fire hisses, as well the tendency for old rush lights (used until modern times in parts of Ireland) to hiss especially before flickering and going out. It is also associated with the appearance of otherworldly creatures e.g. in a story recorded in the National Schools Folklore Collection, Martin Canny of Galway describes how in 1923 two motorists encountered an unnaturally tall man, in old fashioned garb, who bounded onto the car and then, "with a hissing sound, disappeared by jumping straight up into the air."[31] From Meath came the story of two men who went looking for treasure in a fairy fort, only to be confronted and attacked by a hissing half-man, half-bird creature. Hissing swans and "hissing music of the swans," are mentioned, almost as often as hissing creatures from the Otherworld. In one notable story both humming and hissing make an appearance as part of an interaction with the supernatural; while travelling from a dance, a young woman and her sister were accompanied by a neighbour's son for protection.

> *"When passing along the road through The Maghera Farm, they felt a most curious sensation and a most weird humming noise that affected them as if they got a charge of electricity. The weird sensation was followed by a louder hissing sound and one of the girls as if she saw something terrible gave a most hideous shout and grasped the young man and sister with a deathlike grasp"*[32]

This turned out to be a premonition of a death in the family. Hissing tends to be associated with death, with anger and punishment. It does make an appearance in cures, including the following one to cure oral thrush, although I'm not sure I would want anyone trying this one out on me.

*"Thrush: -*
*Catch a gander and make him hiss by twisting his wings, and, when hissing, the bill must be in the child's mouth."*[33]

In magical practice, the use of hissing as a healing mechanism is usually in the form of threatening or scaring away illness or malignant energy. It can be used to express or release anger in hexing spells.

## Chords

Certain chords and chord progressions universally strike the ear as happy, sad, unfinished, discordant and so on. Great orchestral works of the classical era rely on these chord progressions to evoke emotion, and to tell a story through music. Western music traditionally constructed chords in intervals of thirds while modern western classical music has used chords of superimposed intervals of fourths. Composers have pushed and evolved the definition and use of chords in an attempt to provoke a reaction – emotional and intellectual – from the listener.

In Irish music, harmony instruments are a fairly recent addition. Fiddles and Standard D (keyless) flutes or whistles were based on intonation and the overtone series, and the harmony used to accompany traditional music tends to be fairly simple (with exceptions, as Irish folk music embraces newer influences).

Triads and chords containing only roots and fifths are popular. As guitar, bouzouki (in EADG tuning) and banjo entered the scene during the folk revival of the 1960s, interest in chordal accompaniment rather than melodic has grown. As with any music, the effect of chords on the emotions of the listener depends on the perception of them being pleasing, discordant, resolved or unfinished.

In Draíocht Ceoil we sometimes use the word "chord" to symbolize the layering of sounds that have inherent magical power, with words that have inherent magical meaning. To avoid confusion, in this book we will use "chord" in its more ordinary musical sense but do bear in mind that image.

## Drumming

The drum has a special place in the history of human music, being one of the earliest and most fundamental instruments. The earliest documented drums to date are from China, from to 5500-2350 BCE. The earliest *Bodhrán* (fixed frame Irish tambour drum) is attributed to 1500 CE but almost certainly predates that. In modern Irish music the *Bodhrán* drives the tempo of a session but is occasionally a solo or accompanist instrument.

Studies have shown that drumming has a very clear effect on the brain, both for those who regularly drum and those listening to or dancing to drums. For example, the brains of drummers who practice and play regularly have a more efficiently organized motor skills area.[34] Drumming and associated physical exercise improve cognitive function. Studies have shown that playing a musical instrument improves cortical grey matter function including perception, memory, speech, decision making but studies of drummers that concentrate on the "information superhighway" area of the brain, the white matter, found significant differences between them and non-drummers.

Participating in drumming circles can increase natural Killer T Cells that fight viruses, and some cancers. It's important to understand that this doesn't in any way support fraudulent claims that sound therapy can cure cancer, only that on a smaller level it can promote the body's own impulse to heal. Listening to drumming provokes an emotional and physiological result. One of the most interesting is that listening to drumming elicits a response even from damaged areas of the brain.

In terms of Draíocht Ceoil, I would always promote the *Bodhrán* over any other type of drum, because it is part of our culture and heritage, and it is intrinsic to the folk magic practice of Draíocht Ceoil. Obviously, people will use whatever drum suits them and that's okay too. However, if you have the opportunity to incorporate a properly made, handmade Irish *Bodhrán* into your practice do so.

## Pitch

Different pitches were held to have sway over humans, a belief backed by modern science and research. The lowest level of pitch is considered to be discharge sounds, draining and upsetting the listener. The *Filí* of old knew this, and created a low pitched "death chant," (a rather double-edged sword that could kill the hearer, or the person trying to perform it).

Higher pitches provoke feelings of joy and energy. Middle ranges are calm and persuasive. Chants in the middle pitch produce rich, higher energy overtones, combining the qualities of soothing and energy. A range of modern studies from the 1960s onwards supports the ancient belief that people respond in the following way:

***High*** – Music at a high pitch raises the spirit (this is the pitch that "charges" the brain, energizes it).
***Medium*** – Music at a middle pitch tends to persuade and engage both emotional and intellectual responses. In addition, medium pitched notes played or sung together build up to a higher resonance, thus combining soothing tones with energizing properties.
***Medium Low*** – On the lower end of medium pitch, sound can soothe and heal. It has qualities that lull and distract from pain. It is associated with calming people in physical and emotional pain.
***Very Low*** – Very low-pitched notes are associated with upsetting and disrupting, producing discomfort and can be extremely unsettling. It is worth bearing in mind, the lowest chant is the death chant in Old Irish texts on the *Filí*.

All these ways in which music and sound can affect us have led to a body of practices globally that include therapeutic and emotional healing. While not specifically Irish in tradition, they mirror the practice of Draíocht Ceoil and are worth considering here.

## Sound Therapy

Another echo of Draíocht Ceoil in the modern world is found in the growing popularity of Sound Therapy (not to be confused with Music Therapy). This is a rather nebulous term that covers a variety of new age and alternative medicine practices, but ultimately combines sound and music at certain frequencies to attempt to heal the psyche and promote the emotional well-being of the participant. The most popular iteration of this is sound baths, it works on the principle that immersion in certain sounds triggers a relaxation response and contributes to healing. It incorporates many of the principles of Draíocht Ceoil including the use of certain pitches to promote an emotional response. While there are many unqualified, opportunistic people offering sound therapy, the growing understanding of the therapeutic effect of music in a more scholarly setting has improved the field immensely. Psychoacoustics aims to understand and quantify the effect of music on the brain and body.

It should be stressed that Draíocht Ceoil is primarily a magical art, and although healing spells are part of the practice, it is not a therapy, nor should it ever be mistaken for one or presented as one.

There is some scientific evidence to back up the claims of sound therapy and sound baths. While there is little hard data to prove significant physical healing (and people should be skeptical of claims that this practice cures physical conditions) there are interesting studies that demonstrate the overall improvement in well-being emotionally and psychologically. A 2018 randomized controlled study found it lowered anxiety, decreased heart rate variability (which denotes a lowering of stress) and a 2020 study noted a positive mood improvement in the majority of participants using the Positive and Negative Scale (PANAS) and a 2020 meta-analysis of previous studies and data reported that the practice was associated with a general improvement in anxiety and depression, coupled with better pain management (perhaps the most interesting part of the results!) Some evidence emerged that it could lower blood pressure, heart rate and respiratory rate.

Again, this demonstrates the real effect of sound on our bodies and minds. In terms of Draíocht Ceoil it coincides with the ancient belief here in music's properties, to soothe and heal. In a modern practice of Draíocht Ceoil, it can be very useful to experience a sound bath firsthand, to note the effect on us, to try to attune to the frequency used and lean into the experience. You will see described later how to cleanse and recharge the energy of a place using similar methods – resonant, immersive sound.

In addition to the way organized sound can operate on us, a lot can depend on the circumstances in which we receive them.

## Music Therapy

Sound therapy relies on specific sound frequencies to promote healing and well-being, while music therapy is a more standardized discipline that focuses on addressing symptoms like stress and pain. Music therapists undergo standardized training and attain recognized certifications. It is part of the medical field, rather than a spiritual or new age practice and music therapists often work in hospitals, substance abuse treatment centers, or rehab centers as well as private medical practices. A music therapist will identify the "end goal" e.g. to alleviate symptoms of Alzheimer's, to help with depression, to enable the patient to cope with emotions during withdrawal etc. Because it can be tailored to the individual it can be very effective for a wide range of psychological and emotional needs, even in young children. It is a growing field, and as a result we have access to more and more data that underlines the effect of music on our well-being.

## How We Listen

The circumstances in which we receive music also affect how we react. Our ancestors would have experienced the great ceremonial horns of the Bronze Age differently simply because that level of sound was rare and reserved solely for great occasions. Live music strikes us differently than recorded music. A band playing in a large stadium, or a huge orchestral performance is different that hearing a lone singer with a guitar in a small venue. Studies show clear links between communal experience of the work, and positive emotional and intellectual responses.

Our response to music and sound develops continuously throughout life and is affected by personal circumstances, life experience, and education. We will respond differently to different pieces of music and to different sounds, and our response to the same piece will change over time. Sound accumulates associations, both positive and negative, that are unique to us as individuals, but the same can have very different associations for others. Choosing sound can be a balancing act between understanding both the inherent power of the note, melody, chord, word or noise and the power it holds for you specifically.

Experiencing music through headphones can make it an intensely personal experience while experiencing it in a communal setting creates powerful bonds. Fans of any genre of music form friendships over shared emotional and intellectual reactions to music.

One of my fondest memories is of the reunion concert for the band Orchestral Manoeouvres in the Dark, (OMD) who reformed after 20 years in 2006. They kicked off their tour in Dublin, in the Olympia Theatre. I went with low expectations, but what unfolded was an extraordinary and magical confluence of perfect acoustics, and flawless performance. The crowd moved through various phases of engagement, from mild nostalgia to wild enthusiasm. The energy was literally magical, and by the end, complete strangers were hugging each other. No one wanted to leave the venue, lingering well past the last encore. It was a concert we talked about for years after and which entered a kind of legendary state of "Ah, you had to be there."

Covid disrupted the performance of live music in an unprecedented way. Even during World Wars, theatres and concert halls provided relief and escapism, but during the pandemic not only were we deprived of live music, but we were deprived of that communal experience of the same. The solution was found in small, outdoor performances, by local musicians to their communities (harking back to traditions of old) and by the new, technological method – performing on social media and creating a new experience of communal listening. Music in the pandemic was also used to alleviate boredom and isolation – I worked in my music business through-out and we provided a lifeline to many who either revived an interest in learning an instrument or took one up for the first time. I "tuned" violins over Zoom calls and took instruments in over my garden wall to be re-strung. The joy of learning an instrument purely for personal performance made a comeback in this period.

In terms of Draíocht Ceoil, how you choose to express your sound spell will be important. You can choose to be public and loud or private and personal. You can work alone, or in community.

Taking one example: if you are targeting an individual for a healing spell, the person may benefit from having it performed for them in person or being able to experience it through headphones. For spells of public importance, especially political issues and activism, public performance is preferable. Now, you can interpret this in a number of ways, from gathering like-minded individuals and performing together, to seeing it simply as the act of making the sound out loud. In my experience, the more public the performance the more powerful the impact and outcome.

The creation of music and sound can also affect the person making it, and we each bring our individual filters to bear.

## How We Create

We cannot underestimate the effect of creating a sound spell on us, as well as on any desired outcome. A poet conveys personal emotion through their words, and a composer through their music. Whether you are creating a sound spell for a personal issue, or for another individual or for the public well-being, inevitably some part of your own emotion and outlook will be conveyed.

Similarly, the act of playing or singing is a physical act. You are using your voice or body to create sound and to make an impact. Using them to connect to energy, or to manipulate energy, imposes a strain on your physical being.

This book assumes a certain level of basic experience in these matters but it is worth stating that before attempting any working you need to be clear both on the outcome you want and on how much of yourself you are willing to put into it. You have a duty of care to yourself to ensure you have boundaries in place.

Emotion is an important aspect of any creative endeavour, but it can also affect your objectivity. Meditation and journeying can all contribute to the ability to express or harness emotion, in a controlled and effective way. Objectivity is your friend in these matters and the more intensely personal the issue, the more you need to cultivate it.

At this point, I highly recommend starting to practice the exercises given throughout the book. These are solid, repetitive exercises designed to build up your confidence and awareness. Even if you consider yourself to be an experienced magical practitioner, these exercises are valuable as a basis for the specific techniques of this tradition.

## Chapter 5

# Accessing Sound Energy

Having looked at how sound affects us, and how the Irish traditions of music included belief in its magical properties, the next step is understanding how this translates into actual magical practice.

The first step is learning how to access natural magical energy through sound, and how we view that energy and its relationship to ourselves, in this tradition. In Irish traditions, the words given to magical energy or energy found in wild places and in nature is *Brí* and energy derived from human usage and occupation is *Bua*. These are very useful terms, and while their history and etymology are sometimes disputed, the practice of dividing energy into natural and man-made is well established. I use them because they are what I have always used and am used to, and I find that being aware of the type of magical energy you are accessing adds refinement to any working.

### Using Sound to Tune In to Natural Magical Energy

There are two actions in Draíocht Ceoil – *Isteach* (in) and *Amach* (out) and there are two types of sound, Natural (*Brí*)and Human (*Bua*). Most uses of Draíocht Ceoil use both types of action. But *Isteach,* taking inside (physically listening) is the first step in Draíocht Ceoil.

The basic belief in Draíocht Ceoil is that magical energy can be assessed by sound, by tuning into its frequency. When you listen, and take in the natural sound of magic, you attune yourself to it, like an orchestra tunes to whatever pitch is required by the composer. Then when you are in tune, you expel a sound

(*Amach*) that is either on that same pitch or designed to alter the energy to a pitch of your choosing.

I have a handy graphic that I use in my class to illustrate. In it you see the central figure (the practitioner) taking in and attuning to the energy of either a place, or a person (or persons, if dealing with crowd energy). First, we take in the sound energy, then we attune ourselves to it.

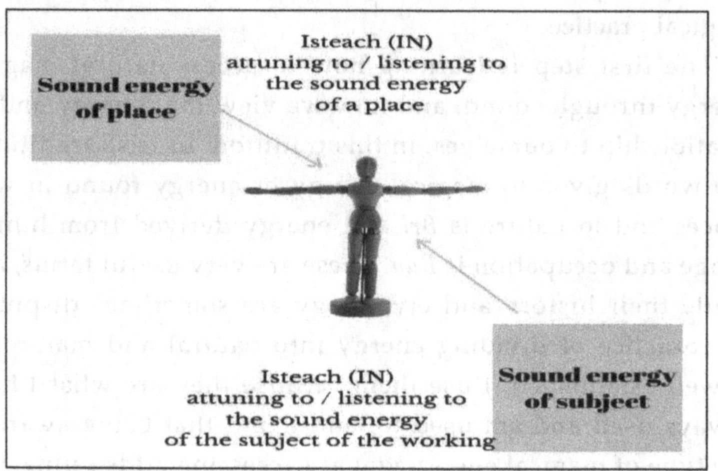


ISTEACH, "INSIDE" (LISTENING) – TAKING IN AND TUNING INTO SOUND

Music is felt in two main parts of the body, head and chest, which I personally think of as corresponding to soul and heart, or one could say, intellect and heart.

*Isteach* requires listening skills, including active listening. There are so many ways in which you can hone your listening skills, from isolating individual sounds in whatever setting in which you find yourself, to eavesdropping shamelessly on people around you. This latter is my favourite, I'm so nosey I have lingered long after my meal was finished or wandered up and down supermarket aisles, just to hear the end of an overheard conversation. As I type this, the ladies at the table next to me are having a highly intriguing conversation about a letter, a phone call and a family scandal. My husband often marvels at my ability to hear the conversation at our table and the one taking place across the room – a benefit of hypersensitivity to sound.

Active listening is not just hearing, though. It is important to nurture our comprehension and processing of what we hear. For many with Neurodivergence this presents a challenge – people speaking too quickly, or being too idiomatic in their speech can cause a delay in processing the actual words. Starting with non-verbal sound is best, and the exercises below should help. Practicing is also important. Even if you only take one sound, one sentence, and try to hear not only the words but the intent behind them, you open yourself up more and more until it becomes second nature. We all suffer from the urge to listen only to hear a gap where we can insinuate ourselves, especially if the topic is interesting to us or we have experience of the subject. It is important to curb this instinct and to be present in the moment. Hear what is being said and just as importantly, hear what is being left unsaid.

### *Exercise*

A simple exercise that can help you experience *Isteach* is to fill a glass of water and listen to the sound the water makes as it fills the space, and how it changes as it nears the top of the glass. Then empty it, close your eyes and repeat. Try to gauge how close it is to the top, before it spills over. Try to fill it as near to the top as possible without spilling.

This is something you can observe every time you fill a glass. Try it with different vessels – pots, pans, the kettle, a sink. Listen to the change in pitch and timbre as the liquid fills the receptacle and try to gauge the amount you need. Listen to the difference between hot and cold water. Yes, there really is a difference! Hot water emits lower frequency sounds and reduces higher frequency ones compared to cold water.

Listen to water in nature, be it rain falling on hard or soft surfaces or the sound of the sea or river. If you have wind chimes, listen to the sound of rain against them, producing secondary notes. If you have a rain drum, a "tongue drum" suitable for outdoor spaces, then I am incredibly jealous and may need to steal it from you.

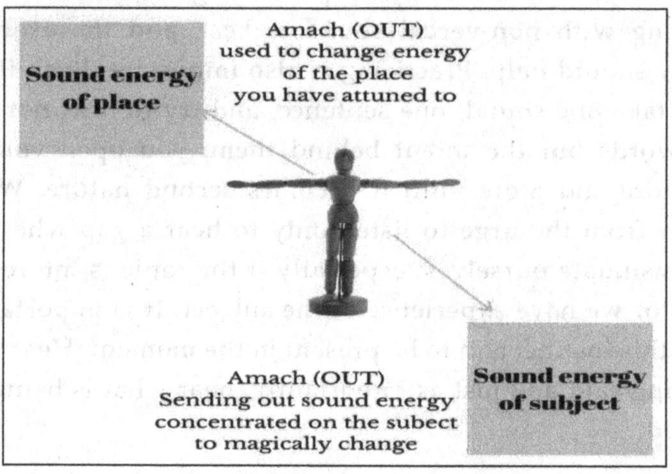


AMACH, "OUT" (MAKING NOISE) -PUSHING SOUND ENERGY OUT TO CREATE CHANGE

When it comes to *Amach*, the practitioner uses the energy to which they are now attuned, to affect magical change. They send back altered sound energy to the place or subject, using sound as the vehicle for change.

### *Exercise*

For *Amach* a simple exercise is to listen to and modulate your own breathing. Take a deep breath in, then expel. Try to alter the sound of the breath in different ways – through your teeth, hissed out, through pursed lips like a breathy whistle and so on. Again, you can do this as an ongoing exercise, to remind yourself of the principles involved. Adjust volume, timbre and rhythm.

Experiment with volume, by dropping from loud to quiet, working your way up gradually through levels of volume, or matching rhythm to volume (e.g. staccato while quiet, largo with loud and so on,) while remaining at the same pitch.

When in conversation, deliberately match your volume and tempo to the other person. Mirror their speech – side note: don't go too far and start imitating their accent, this can lead to misunderstandings and accusations of taking the mickey.

Note the ways in which you make sound in everyday activities. For example, the click-click of the keyboard as you type, any tics such as tapping pens or drumming fingernails on a hard surface. These are ways in which your body expresses emotions of which you may not even be conscious. Why does your body erupt in sound this way – are you stressed, nervous, excited?

As an aside, dyspraxia runs in my family, and often these fidgets are a way of rooting oneself in time and space. Proprioceptive feedback tells your brain where your foot is, where your hand is, in relation to the world around you and when these signals are slow or absent, we fidget to replace them. The creation of noise in doing so is an interesting aspect.

Build on these exercises by paying attention to every small daily sound. If you are already sensitive to sound, you may be more used to filtering out sound rather than focusing on it. If you have been happily ignoring the many tiny noises that fill up our day-to-day existence, start paying attention now. We should also become used to categorizing the type of energy these sounds represent e.g. the sound of a zipper or the creak of a floorboard are examples of *Bua* sounds while birdsong, the sound of the wind, leaves rustling and insects humming are

*Brí* sounds. Practice tuning into them, filtering them, listening for them.

When you enter a space, take a few moments to listen to it. Hear the sounds that are normal for that space. Note any sounds that are unusual for it, or unwelcome, or that strike you as odd. Note your emotional and intellectual reaction to the individual sounds, and to the overall "noise" of the space.

Make notes. You can write down your observations or indeed, record them on voice notes or short videos. But give yourself a body of work to look back on, both to build on areas you find difficult and recognize your strengths and also, simply to see how far you have come.

## The Song of Place

Bearing in mind that the world in which we live has become exponentially louder, with human-created noise, than at any other time in history, we are overwhelmed daily with auditory input. The sheer volume of information we take in daily, from announcements, radio, even listening to traffic to hear what's coming at us, all has to be processed. This can make it hard to suddenly start actively listening.

Each place has a different inherent sound. I call it the "song of place." This song can be based on *Brí* (the natural energy of a place) or *Bua* (the energy a place accumulates through human usage. Crowd energy also falls under *Bua*).

One type of energy or "Song" is not better than another, just different. But in my experience, people find nature more accessible than trying to start in *Bua* energy. The clearest energy to access tends to be in places with higher *Brí*. Ideally, we want somewhere wild, with minimal human occupation, however, if you don't happen to have a handy cliff, or accessible mountain top just find the quietest place you can. Because all music is based on the natural Harmonic Series, I would recommend starting in nature, but nature can be your garden, a local park, some patch of green. You may not be able to find perfect peace, but you can find a quiet time of day.

There is no such thing as true silence, in my opinion. Certainly, if you are sensitive to sound you will know that in the quietest place, there is sound. There is resonance, vibration, energy. The idea is not to achieve perfect silence, but to listen through the layers of sound to actually "hear" magical energy.

## Tuning Fork

Most people with an interest in Draíocht Ceoil will have some interest in music and will know what a tuning fork is. A tuning fork is two-pronged, made of a metal like steel (an elastic metal), with U shaped tines, and acts as an acoustic resonator when struck off a hard surface. Tuning forks are also used in medicine, to test hearing and check bone fractures. It is often used in the field of neurology. The Rydel-Seiffer tuning fork test involves placing the instrument on areas like ankles, where there is bone underneath. If the patient doesn't feel any vibration, there may be neuropathy. They are also used to aid relaxation and are a part of the growing field of sound therapy.

I use the analogy of a tuning fork to help people access the natural magical energy around them. If strike a tuning fork and place it on a surface to resonate, you can feel the vibration even as you hear the note produced. When you reach out for magical energy, you are the tuning fork, and the vibration of energy resonates through your body and the sound emits from you. This sound will be the song of that place.

If you have difficulty in seeing yourself as a conduit for vibrations and sound, if possible, check out somewhere near you that does sound baths, or sound therapy. Gongs, steel drums and the modern Swiss instrument, the Hang, or handpans are excellent for experiencing deep vibrations.

Tambour drums like the *Bodhrán,* are useful, but to feel a full vibration throughout your body might need a louder, deeper toned, strongly resonating instrument. It depends on how easily you feel vibrations. I have students who experience it by being near speakers blasting out heavy metal. Ruinous for your hearing but great for getting the idea of quivering in response to sound energy. Another found themselves finally understanding it at a classical concert, as the full blast of orchestral music swept over an auditorium. There is no wrong way.

*Exercise*

This is one of the moments where you should probably sit and think about this for a while. Imagine yourself sitting somewhere that draws you; it is peaceful, no distractions. You start to listen and at first you hear only the surface noise. Then you begin to isolate each sound, listening to each in turn. Then you begin to hear the underlying, simpler, tones – the natural vibration of the place. Its own song. (This is "*Isteach*", going inside, listening).

At this point, you "strike" off that vibration, and allow your body to attune to it. It rises through you; you open your mouth and allow out whatever bubbles up. (This is "*Amach*" – outside, sending out energy).

Practicing this in your mind before attempting it in reality can help remove the self-consciousness or doubt that can be a stumbling block to trying any new technique. When it comes time to try it, the key is patience. Some people find it easy; others find it hard but just like learning a piece of music, it doesn't matter how long it takes as long as you can do it well in the end.

## Preparation

Other techniques to practice before you try to approach a place and tune into it are visualization – many of you will be familiar with this and others will not. Visualization is simply the ability to imagine yourself or imagine events or outcomes. To create a clear picture of the same in your mind, and hold it in place, usually while thinking of the desired outcome and the steps needed to achieve it (both magically and mundanely).

Meditation is also a useful tool. I practice the traditional method of Immramic Meditation[35] and the Irish Pagan School offers excellent courses in a related Irish form of active journeying. These techniques are invaluable as a base for all kinds of spell casting, active magical practices, and also for spiritual practices.

## Music and Musical Instruments

Listening to your favourite music, especially a familiar piece, is a perfect way to practice the techniques needed. Anyone who has done music theory – or indeed, music as a subject for a school or music examination board – will be familiar with the practice of listening to orchestral music and separating out the various instruments by section, following their line of melody in a score. As you listen, choose one instrument (voice, guitar, fiddle, drums, trumpet – it doesn't matter which) and follow it to the exclusion of the others. If it stops, listen until you can pinpoint the moment it rejoins the others. If it deviates from the main melody, follow it and try to sing along with it.

If you sing in a choir, you will be familiar with harmonies and counterpoints. If you have had limited musical experience, you might like to seek out videos of choirs and listen to (and watch) how the various sections (Soprano, Alto, Tenor and Bass, also known as SATB) interact. Barber shop quartets are another great example of this, and sometimes easier to follow than complex orchestral scores to start with.

I am assuming a love of, if not an education in, music on the part of my readers – otherwise, why be interested in Draíocht Ceoil? If your interest lies more in the use of words, bear in mind that words are in themselves lyrical and musical. The rise and fall of them, the lilting of an accent, and their rhythm, are what attract us to a language.

Listen to music. Listen to as diverse a range of music as possible and reach outside your own preferences. Learning to listen to a sound that is alien, or difficult for you to interpret, is as important as listening to sound that attracts you.

All these techniques will help you tune into the sound of a place and should be practiced as an ongoing part of your Draíocht Ceoil.

## Respect

When you approach a place and try to tune into that magical energy, you have to show respect. In Irish traditions, we believe that we share this reality with things we cannot see. A belief in supernatural entities like the Sí, *Púca*, or *Oilliephéist* living beside us, occupying liminal spaces such as the Dúns and raths that litter the landscape, is embedded in Irish culture. Even today, more than half the population believes in ghosts and fairies, and interestingly the figures are highest in the most populated urban centre, Dublin. Traditionally, these entities have to be shown respect – stories abound of people whose carelessness or arrogance led them to neglect this and who suffered a sharp punishment as a result.

One such example is found in the National Folklore Collection:[36]

> *"There was a boy coming from school once upon a time and he lifted a flag from the place and went off with it. Before long a voice cried after him and said, "Don't take that stone or we will send you home riding on a cow." The boy disobeyed the request of the fairly and the fairy lifted a piece of weed and changed it into a cow and the boy found himself riding on it. He was taken all over the Country. He said he would never go near any thing belonging to the fairy mound again."*

The message time and again is clear – do not disturb this place, do not intrude upon us. You are seeking to share the space, not – and this is crucial – not to invoke, harness or interfere with any other entity within the space.

Raths, Dúns, ancient sites are not suitable places to start. You are interfering with something you don't have any right to access. Similarly for those outside Ireland, do not intrude on indigenous sacred spaces. *Find* a space that is open to all, and approach it respectfully. This may involve visiting several times to establish a bond. It would behoove you to ask permission, leave a gift (something biodegradable and not harmful to plants or wildlife) and then…wait for a response. Asking does not confer permission.

We are an entitled species, used to intruding ourselves into spaces and while previous generations had far more sensitivity to taboo areas, modern humans tend to feel hard done by at the mere suggestion of refusal. Let it go. If a place doesn't want you, no good will come of forcing your way in. Once you feel sure that the place is open to you, then it is time to actively try to connect to the energy there.

Some readers will have their own reliable method of tuning into energy. It is still worth doing the following because the point isn't merely to sense energy but to tune into specifically magical sound energy through Draíocht Ceoil. This is the very first block on which we will build our practice.

Let's take two examples – one, a natural wild environment and the other a quiet spot that is in the centre of human activity. Both will have different energy, different hurdles to navigate but the essentials will remain the same.

## Brí

For the purposes of this exercise, we'll pretend you have arrived at a beautiful, wild place, full of natural *Brí* energy. A high cliff, with brooding mountains at its back, overlooking the Atlantic Ocean, waves crashing against jagged rocks far beneath you. The only sounds are those of nature. The wind, birdsong, the rustle of foliage, the rhythmic beat of the waves, all creating layers of noise. You have established a bond with this place, you are a welcome visitor – now it's time to sit and listen.

First, you are aware of the overall energy of the place. There is a charge in the air, a sense of freedom and vitality. You could scream and howl and the wind would just whip the noise away and throw it out over the sea, or up to the clouds. Your heart beats a little faster, your senses are a little heightened.

But as you wait, and listen, you begin to separate out the different instruments of this wild orchestra. The high screech of a seagull, the relentless beat of the water, the sighs or howls of the wind. These form chords, of low, medium and high notes.

Beneath all of these though, is the base note, the natural note on which all other sounds are based. Whether a sound is discordant or pleasing, is based on their relationship to this note – something we register unconsciously but strongly. This is the note we seek.

When you hear it, the vibrations of it will resonate through your body, and out of your mouth. Right now, is a good time to say – it doesn't matter if you can sing like a nightingale or croak like a frog. If what comes out of your mouth is a squawk is not important, only that the note was clear in your head.

It takes time to be able to hear it, and it takes repeated practice to be proficient at accessing it. But practice not only enables you to access that note but will make it easier and easier to do it again and in other places.

### Bua

You are living in an urban setting, and accessing a wild natural place is not practical for you; this is the experience of many people and as an urban pagan myself, I can assure you there is just as much magical energy in any urban setting as in the wild. It's just a bit different and the sounds you'll encounter vary – but the technique is basically the same. As in the wild, do not assume that you have a right to enter any space – we share this reality with the unseen, even in our cities. Respect is still the key and do not ignore any feelings of resistance to your presence.

Magical energy in an urban environment is different from the energy you get in a wild one, but equally valid and useful. Any practitioner of Draíocht Ceoil needs to be able to tune into both and utilize both. The "sound" is different, and there are two strains of energy within an urban setting. The first is the background *Bua,* the inherent energy created by human occupation of a place. The second is the energy of the people themselves, not as individuals but as a collective, which I personally term the energy of crowds. This provides a different base note to either *Brí* or *Bua* and can be a very useful element in your practice.

Tuning into the energy *Bua* is very similar to *Brí* – once you are confident that you are in a safe and grounded relationship with the place, you set about listening, separating out sounds and going deeper each time until you feel that base note. Now, the "*Amach*" part of this might be trickier. Letting a shriek out of you in a busy shopping centre might not be ideal. People are apt to get the wrong idea. But you can do it in the privacy of your own head. As you practice, you will tap into local energy very easily, and without such conscious effort but starting off it is important not to cut corners. Do the task. Listen and listen and wait. It doesn't matter how many tries it takes, getting the basics right is the same as getting good technique at bowing, or learning scales.

As I write this, I am sitting in a cafe in my small local shopping centre. Half the tables are occupied, it is mid-afternoon on a Monday in the middle of school holidays. It is located on a mezzanine, with a balcony overlooking the main part of the shopping centre. When I walked in, there was a wall of noise – the background noises of the shops, and shoppers mixed with piped music, the noise of the kitchen and people talking.

Sometimes people wonder why writers like to write in such an environment, but many of us do. I have written six fiction novels, innumerable poems and this book in small cafes against a backdrop of noise and bustle. (In fairness, a lot of the poems were written in pubs under much more raucous circumstances!)

When I open my laptop, after the ritual arranging of phone, coffee, snack, tray and computer on the cramped table space, and stare at the page, my mind begins to separate the noise into songs, into energy. The hum of the coffee machines echoes the rattle of trolleys across the tiled concourse beneath me, the clink of cutlery is the counterpoint to the rise and fall of voices, the melody of local accents washing over me punctuated by a bell-like "ping" from the cash desk. Beneath me, the energy rises and falls, frenetic and weary by turns but here, above them all the *Bua* is that of an oasis. The energy is charged, yes, but positively – it is relief at sitting down, delight in cream buns and tea, excitement at gossip and beside me, on one side a table of teens playing at being cool, and adult, and on the other a young mam and her baby who thinks the entire place is great craic.

There are some constant notes – the lady at the counter who calls out "Next," and her colleague who sings back, "Tea or coffee, love?" Every time I come here, it is both a familiar melody and a new variation. After a while, I no longer even consciously register this, but I would notice its absence, or the introduction of some alien, discordant element.

As I write, I am not distracted by silence, or by random noise breaking the hush, as I would be if I attempted this in a library, or in a quiet room. My misophonic brain is contrary to the point of weaponizing silence and peace against me. But here, the dense intricacy of sound provides protective layers. This will not be true for everyone, but I offer it as a reminder that you can find the song in any setting and find your place among the notes.

A great place to start in an urban setting is a park. In my classes on Urban Paganism, I talk about city parks as liminal spaces. They combine an element of *Brí* with *Bua* and are an intersection between nature and man. For many city dwellers it is a good setting for exercises in listening and tuning – and because it has an element of *Brí* it will help you with wilder spaces.

## The Energy of Crowds

If you've ever struggled down a busy street with two handfuls of shopping bags, you will be well aware of the energy of a crowd. It can be joyous, cheerful, and comforting or it can be unpredictable, dangerous and angry. Often, it can contain elements of all these things at the same time.

Many people find crowds overwhelming, and develop instinctual habits of protecting themselves, consciously or unconsciously. This is especially true for neurodivergent people. As a child, my go-to solution was humming – something that drove my siblings to distraction. But humming enabled me to feel more aligned with what was happening around me, especially in crowds. While the culprit can be bright lights, multi-sensory marketing techniques, and other irritants, the constant noise and claustrophobic pressure of other people all around you are important factors.

Learning to become more in tune with the energy produced by crowds has twofold benefits. It will make navigating the experience easier, but it also is a powerful source of energy that can be used to protect yourself, or indeed, simply used as magical energy.

## Tapping Into the Energy of Crowds

The shifting and changing music of a crowd can be harder to pinpoint and separate than the sounds you get in either a wild or urban environment and this can pose challenges.

You don't have the same luxury of time to practice, as well as the fact that it's constantly changing. Some people have a natural talent in this regard, a knack for bypassing the slower techniques of static listening but for most people it's best to build up experience and confidence in *Brí* and *Bua* first. Whatever route you take, do what feels comfortable for you. If you try to tune into a crowd energy and find it doesn't work, you can simply try again and again as you improve in general practice. There's no harm in trying.

If you are approaching this as a novice my advice is to set a clear goal. You can use crowd energy to feel safer and better able to exist within that crowd, and to protect yourself from any dangerous shifts in the crowd energy. This should be your first objective. The next phase is learning to harness that energy, and that can wait until you can confidently tap into it.

As ever the primary action is "*Isteach*" – to listen, and to feel the song. Now considering one of the reasons you're probably feeling uncomfortable to start with is the volume and diversity of sound, this can feel like an impossible task. The solution lies in practicing before you ever get into the crowd!

All the techniques mentioned above under Preparation should be borne in mind as well as some special techniques below. If being immersed in a crowd is too problematic, you can do the following while remaining adjacent to the bustle and noise.

Understanding the energy of crowds requires listening and opening oneself to the shifts and movements in that energy. You should know how to ground yourself and protect yourself before approaching the unpredictable and multilayered energy produced by large numbers of individuals in one place.

My favourite technique is to view the crowd as an orchestra, and to start by listening to the noise as if it was an orchestral score, using the same techniques of isolating one sound and following it. Voices, traffic, music, everything that comes together to create the music of a group. Beneath this, you can hear more subtle sounds – individual conversations, muttering, shouts. You can see interaction within the crowd, conversations and calls between groups, and you can hear links between the group and external concerns – phone calls, in particular, linking the crowd to something outside its own concerns.

To protect yourself within a crowd, choose a song you find comforting. Practice it at home, while holding the intent that this is a protective sound, one that will surround you and create a space around you. Then, while in the hustling and movement of a crowd, breath in. Expel the breath while humming, whistling or singing this tune. Breath in, expel the notes, over and over. Visualize it creating a shield of sound energy around you. If you can't sing or hum out loud, do it in your mind.

The sound energy of a crowd varies from group to group. A crowd of shoppers are united by their interest in the goods on display, concerned with moving from shop to shop. Outside of that common goal, there is little to unite the disparate individuals within it. A crowd at a concert, or at a protest or rally, is more cohesive and bound together by a purpose – less open to outside influence, less easily distracted but easier to read.

Once you feel confident that you can attune to crowd energy, you can do more than just protect yourself. You can harness this vibrant energy and use it to fuel a working. The circumstances in which this would occur are varied, perhaps a need to redirect or diffuse the energy surges or a need for a handy burst of energy. You can find the dominant note, change it, or use it, as suits your needs.

## Individual Energy

Every living thing is part of the universal sound. Just like every place, we have our own inherent sound. Each of us has an internal sacred landscape, filled with magical energy. We are part of the cosmos, and we have our own song, as beautiful as the Cat's Eye Nebula.

It is not our place to draw on another's energy just as you should not impose your will on another. Consent is all important – you have no right to interfere with another human being, unless in self-defense. You never have a right to leech off them. You should also carefully protect your own energy from both intrusion and theft.

However, if asked to do a healing for a person, or if asked to use our intuition to read for them, we need to attune to their energy. This is done with consent, and respectfully, in the same way that we approach a space with respect.

The richest source of individual energy is yourself. The three realities in Imrammic meditation are The Otherworld, this reality and your inner sacred landscape[37] – within our own inner landscape, we contain a whole and mystical realm, filled with energy. When we are in tune with the natural energy around us, we enrich our own energy. The practice of meditation – of any type – is invaluable in allowing us to access this but Imrammic Meditation is particularly well suited, a tradition based on the Eachtraí and Immrama literature. This is a body of literature that tells stories of journeys – in both the Pagan and Christian tradition – where the hero encounters beings, magical places, wonders and to some degree, attains some spiritual or magical goal. Both the *Voyage of Bran* and *The Voyage of (Saint) Brendan* are examples of the Immrama.

## Chapter 6

# Using Sound as Magic

We have explored the first step – accessing or tuning into magical energy. Now it is time to discuss what to do with it once we've got it!

The point of Draíocht Ceoil is to use sound, including words, to enable you to create effective magical workings. It can be used to create planned, carefully constructed work or alternatively to react quickly and instinctively to situations. We will explore both in detail but in this chapter, let's take an overview of what this entails.

The inherent energy of a place, both wild energy and human energy, fuels the magical working. In Draíocht Ceoil, we interpret this through the natural "base note" created by this magical energy. Now you can take in this note, it is time for the "*Amach.*" The choice is now to either use that note to create a spell (complex or simple) or to alter that note to change the source energy itself.

### Using the Base Note

An unaltered base note is usually done to fuel workings, either as the source of energy for immediate change (e.g. to protect yourself quickly) or long lasting, nuanced work for long term changes. The base note can be drawn from the place you're in at the time, or from your inner landscape.

If you are familiar with music, you will understand the concept of chords and harmonies. I like to think of building a spell as taking the basic note and building a chord on it, or sometimes, creating a melody and harmonizing with it. We use music, words, and other sounds all together to create these layers, adding depth to and amplifying our intention.

The more aware you become of the sound of the spaces in which you find yourself, the more easily you can access it, even if in an unfamiliar place. This becomes easy through practice. If you work daily, it can become second nature.

You also carry notes within yourself, within your own sacred landscape. If you practice meditations like Immrama, designed to connect you to your inner world, you can create a space within you, that can be accessed at any time. You can create and hold base notes there for your needs. For example, if you have an ongoing need for healing or protection, connect with a space within that helps with that. Spend time building that space, and visualizing it, and hum or sing that note repeatedly.

Once you have your base note, you can use it in many ways. You can use it as the start point for a simple melody or chant. You can harmonize with it or build chords around it. If you are familiar with chord progression, certain chords provoke an almost universal emotional reaction, creating music that is generally held to be sad, happy, uplifting, discordant and so on. Accessing and using the base note is the basis of the art of Draíocht Ceoil.

## Changing the Base Note

This would be done to change the energy of a place (e.g. cleansing) or in crowds, to change the atmosphere and neutralize problems. It is also to raise energy and positively charge it (when the inherent base note doesn't suit your needs, but the energy is potent).

It is important to understand that harmonizing with a base note is not the same as changing it. Harmonizing is using that note as a starting point, and complementing it with other sound, designed to raised complex rich layers of magical energy.

Changing the base note is literally altering the inherent sound of the energy of a place or gathering. Doing that to a place is difficult. Doing it to a crowd is easier – gatherings and crowds are temporary and made up of constantly shifting energy whereas a place has an inherent, fixed tone. Crowds can be easily manipulated through music, and this makes the energy of a crowd more malleable, even when you are using your more subtle personal use of sound rather than blasting music from speakers.

Changing the energy of a place is a different proposition. When doing cleansing of a place, whether one of *Brí* or *Bua* energy, what we often find is that we are restoring the original energy that has been altered or tainted through usage. It can sometimes be like tuning a piano, that has slowly gone out of tune through years of playing or sometime like tuning a violin that has gone suddenly and catastrophically out of tune due to a violent change in temperature or a sharp knock. When a place suffers either long-term, slow, contamination or sudden upheaval, the energy changes. Cleansing through Draíocht Ceoil restores it to its natural, inherent pitch.

More unusual is the need to change the natural note. It can happen when the area is being repurposed – a building used for industrial or commercial use turned into residential, for example. In this instance, simply cleansing the energy is not sufficient. I have worked on apartments created in old warehouses and factories, where the energy simply is not conducive to relaxation or sleep.

When a place has a reputation for being unlucky, it often means one needs to restore it to an earlier, or more natural note but in some cases the inherent note is simply "off." It's like walking into a room and being affected by ultra-low frequencies without realizing it. You can feel the discomfort without perhaps knowing the cause. If a place has an inherently inhospitable note you have to ask yourself, do I need to be here? Remember what was said earlier about respect for a place – we are not entitled to be in every space. But if the answer is yes, then you need to tackle the root cause. No amount of cleansing will cure this problem. It takes weeks, sometimes months of steady work to change a base note like that, but it will be worth it.

Remember we are not "banishing" nor are we seeking to impose ourselves on the space. This work involves respectful, slow attuning to the place's sound energy, learning its song, and singing it into a better, more hospital energy. Again, this is a rare occurrence – most bad energy comes from *Bua*, from human usage, and can be cleansed and most places with inhospitable energy are not places we need to be!

## Electronics and Magic

Technology has enabled us not only to hear new sounds – as in the case of the Cat's Eye Nebula – but to create sounds or reproduce sounds. The average electronic keyboard can render the sound of any instrument and more advanced models can mimic orchestras. Similarly, one can create a range of noises from beeps to car alarms using technology. New instruments such as the Theremin (invented in 1928 by Louis Theremin) provide unique, eerie sounds.

I have often been asked can these sounds be used in Draíocht Ceoil and the answer is a resounding yes. My eldest child has recently taken up trumpet and now that he has progressed beyond the "cow lowing in distress" stage, I have recorded several notes for use in workings. Similarly, I have birdsong, waves and other sounds on my phone, which help me set the base note for workings. You really are only limited by your imagination. Use any instrument or sound making equipment at your disposal. If you have a Theremin, I am jealous, and please send me videos of you using it in Draíocht Ceoil. If you have any weird and wonderful noise maker, get it out and use it to the fullest.

## Tradition versus Modernity

Using culturally rooted instruments is always a good choice – the *Bodhrán* trumps the Djembe in Draíocht Ceoil, simply because the former is so closely related to folk music, to agriculture (originating as a winnowing frame) and to Irish cultural practices. But if you only have an instrument that is culturally meaningful to you, you can, of course, use it. Draíocht Ceoil is an inherently joyful, creative practice and rigid rules about how to make and create do not suit us. Acknowledge the unique sound that traditional instruments bring, be aware that their use helps you to build your own practice with a nod to its cultural roots. But don't be afraid to use anything that enables you to create sound and magic.

I use a lot of traditional Irish instruments and especially I use traditional Irish musical and poetic forms. However, one of my favourite tools for hexing is a green plastic Kazoo. I am obsessed with Theremins and Hang Drums. The Hang Drum is another modern instrument, based on the Trinidad Steel Drum, and developed by Felix Rohner and Sabina Schärer in Switzerland, 2001. It is made of specially constructed steel, in a "flying saucer" shape, with tonal panels that emit different notes when struck. Although new, the Hang is wonderfully suited to Draíocht Ceoil as is its close cousin, the Rain Drum (a Hang-type percussion steel drum that you leave outside and allow the rain to "play" as it hits off it).

If you can have any source of sound that adds depth and power to your working, use it. Some people will gravitate more towards voice and words, others towards music and sound. Some will be drawn to natural sound and others to electronics and manipulated sound. It is all part of the whole.

## Using Non-Lexical Vocal Sound

In Draíocht Ceoil, humming and related sound making (what my poor mother calls "mouth noises" i.e. the disturbing range of noises from clicks to "*la la la*" that all inventive kids can produce at will) are tools of the trade. As important as it is to practice "*Isteach,*" to listen, it is equally important to gain confidence in "*Amach*," in using your voice as an instrument. You need absolutely zero actual music ability to tap into this – it's about resonance and pitch. Make high pitched sound, low pitched sound, be guttural, be sharp – move your tongue around your mouth and make a sound.

Playing around with non-lexical sound is also an opportunity to play with volume. You can make slight, breathy, whispery sounds, or you can hum at full volume. Practice running up and down pitch, raising and lowering volume, dropping from loud to quiet and back again for dramatic effect. All these techniques will add to your workings, to your performance and amplification of magical energy.

It is vital to be aware of how to make sound, rather than just how to hear it. This does not mean you have to be a great or even competent musician. It does mean that you should enjoy sound, be sensitive to it, and be prepared to make it.

The simplest exercise in *Amach* is something that occurs every day, in a host of small ways. It is in your tone of voice, your pitch and tempo, when interacting with other people. There is little point in a practice that you reserve for "special occasions." You have to use it in your daily life. Be aware of how you talk to the shop assistant, the waiter, the person you encounter in the queue. Watch how they react to your sound energy. If you speak kindly, if you inject *Suantraí* or *Geantraí* into your voice, listen for the corresponding tones in theirs. Listen to the strain beneath angry or stressed sound energy, can you hear *Goltraí*? Is it fueled by sorrow, rather than meanness?

We can bring out the sound energy we want to see in others by projecting it ourselves. This is at the heart of *Amach*.

## Aiming

Once you have raised magical energy, you need to actually aim it at something or someone. Every step along the way is done with this in mind.

You have identified a need. While this may seem obvious, you'd be surprised how often people neglect to select a clear, specific target. When we feel strongly, we are inclined to just pour that emotion into a working, but it's wasted if we don't place a structure around it. What exactly is the root of the issue?

You must examine the situation in detail and identify the desired outcome. Sometimes even well-meaning interference can backfire. Unless you have looked at everything, including possible repercussions to you, or others, you will have unintended results. You need to plot a clear path between the root cause of the issue, to the desired outcome, and express both as clearly as possible.

You then choose the sounds needed to create this outcome. We will obviously go into that in much greater detail but again, preparation is key.

You will refine your working until only the desired outcome is targeted. Don't forget to take one last breath, and think, before acting. You don't want to waste any of the precious, hard-earned magical energy by not being specific.

Whether you are performing a simple spell or a complex layered working, the basic steps above need to be ticked off. If you are reacting from anger, fear or panic, the temptation to skip steps, to lash out without care, can be overwhelming. If you are working quickly, you can still follow these steps if you have practiced until it's second nature.

Next, you take aim and fire. In Draíocht Ceoil we use pitch, resonance and volume, tempo and words to pinpoint our target and hit it square on.

Pitch as seen in previous chapters has an effect ranging from healing and uplifting, to depressing or disturbing depending on whether you use high, low or medium pitch. Changing between pitches and layering pitch can be used to emphasize important words, or phrases, or to add emotional tension to your piece.

Volume adds dramatic effect and can be used to build to a crescendo or drop to a whisper. Like pitch, this provides emphasis, drama and provokes an emotional reaction. Volume can also change the way pitch affects us. High notes may charge the brain but if too loud, actually act as an irritant. Low notes can be disturbing or healing, depending on volume. You can use silence to create a boundary around the spell, and to emphasize some aspects of the working. If the need is simple, the spell can be simple. Simple magic is powerful too. What counts the most is knowing what you need, choosing the right sounds to achieve it and performing the spell with the end result firmly in mind.

### *Exercise*

Play with pitch and volume separately. Listen to different notes at high, medium and low pitch. Practice singing or humming at that pitch or playing the notes on your instruments.

Listen to music or speech at different volumes. How low do you have to turn it down for it to stop being coherent? How loud before you find it intolerable? Note both your physical and emotional response to each.

Now combine both pitch and volume. Play the lowest note you can at high volume, the effect can be startling! Try out different pitches at different volumes, not excluding whispering or shouting at either extreme, and note your individual reaction to each. Again, pay attention to both your physical and emotional reactions.

## Whisper, Song, Roar

When we talk about the "volume" of a spell in Draíocht Ceoil, we mean several things. Firstly, it can mean the degree to which we amplify it – how much sound energy we put into it. It can also refer to the volume at which we perform it. In this practice, the traditional shorthand for both is "Whisper, Song, Roar."

As part of spell construction, the volume of a spell can be whisper, song or roar or a mix of them. Take, for example, a healing spell – the ailment may strike you as needing coaxing (whisper) charming (song) or beating into submission (roar). Similarly, a protection spell may involve a gentle (whisper) persuasive (song) or very firm and direct (roar) action.

Another expression of "Whisper, Song, Roar," is how public or private a working is. A Whispered spell is private and intimate, a Song or Roar is public, or in the public interest. Some workings are very much in the public realm. Rosc poetry was traditionally composed for important, public, issues including legal judgment, battle magic and political statements. Rosc spells always come under the public category of "Roar."

Workings for some personal, private end are classed as Whisper. Good luck songs, sowing and churning songs and labouring tunes would be designated as "Song." While they are personal to the farmer or worker, a good harvest or good yield of milk also benefits the community. Some magical music lay between private and fully public, for example, a young girl might sing about wanting a lover in a group of women but not in wider company.

Knowing both the appropriate volume for each part of your spell, as well as whether it is a private, semi-private or public issue, helps make it clear, direct and targeted.

Tempo is another important element. There are several ways in which we can use speed effectively. When you are raising the energy to create magic, you can use a steadily increasing tempo to reach a crescendo at the correct moment. You can also switch from fast to slow to create change and drama within the working.

Tempo affects words as much as music. Think of modern rappers, and their fast, staccato delivery, the way they can convey defiance or anger through tempo. Contrast this to lullabies, laments, and keening which can manipulate emotions and facilitate their release. If you are trying to convey a sense of urgency, or outrage, a slow tempo will hinder you. If you want to convey deliberate intent or strength, it may be appropriate. The more you experiment with Tempo, the better a sense you'll develop of what works and when.

For example, if working with the Rosc (a magical poetic form) a traditional technique is to set your Rosc poem within a body of prose to emphasize it. It changes the tempo and rhythm of performance from the prose to the Rosc section and back again, adding another layer to the power and intensity of the poem. It also makes the central point or target of your working stand out. (See Chapter 8 for an in-depth exploration of the Rosc as magical poetry).

## Opening and Closing

In many Irish poetic forms, including Rosc, we see the concept of "*Dúnadh*" which uses the same lines to open and close a poem, encasing the message within a boundary. The same concept is used to create the overall working in Draíocht Ceoil; ideally the entire spell is created with the same opening and closing lines, actions, notes etc. Whether you are creating something simple or complex, the principle remains the same. Using *Dúnadh* also sets boundaries around the practitioner. In Wicca, the use of physically drawn circles for ritual or spell casting is common. In Irish folk magic, there is no such traditional practice but the more subtle use of *Dúnadh* helps to create a safe space and to ensure magical energy remains enclosed, and targeted.

Interestingly, the poetic art of *Dúnadh* is mirrored in many reels in Folk music – where the piece ends on a note designed to lead one back to the beginning of the piece. Many poetic forms in Irish use the last word of one line to open the next, and so on, creating spirals of words. In fact, everywhere you look in Irish music and poetry, you can see examples of this practice. It's a very simple and effective way to combine tradition with your own composition.

## Structuring and Building Spells

Bringing all these elements together can seem daunting at first, but you can start off with a simple form and then practice and experiment.

The basic technique used to create any working is common sense. After that what is mainly required is patience and an understanding of what sound and structure will suit your requirements. Think back to what you've learned about music and sound. If you know what music suits the situation, you are halfway there. You can use an existing piece of music that you feel is suitable or put together your own sound. You could put your own words to a favourite melody. You can choose to use bells, *Bodhrán*, or electronic sounds. There are many tools at your disposal, so sit down and think it through. One of my favourite techniques is to use sound without words until the halfway point and then introduce chanting or verse, building up to a crescendo at the end.

Set out clear goals for your working. For example, if trying to create a protection spell, you need to identify clearly what you mean by protection, and from what or whom do you require it? What medium will you use – song, poetry, non-melodic sounds? What pitch and rhythm suit it? Write it down and refine it. Be as streamlined as possible.

Another question that it is important to ask yourself is how long should the working last? Different issues require more or less time. Ten or twenty seconds is generally insufficient as it doesn't allow enough time for the sound energy to take effect. I find three to five minutes perfect. Experimenting will show you what works best for you. Some things are best dealt with in a short, sharp way and others require nuance and time. Experience and experimentation will teach you what works best for you.

Example:

Taking the example of a healing spell. State a clear intent (Avoid open-ended or vague intent. "Heal" is too vague. "To aid with post operative recovery," is good. "To promote a clean, infection-free healing from X operation," is better again). then choose your sound.

Let us say we have gone the route of using individual notes from a medium to low pitch. If you have an electronic keyboard, these can be easy to produce in long, extended reverberation. Tuning forks from 432hz downwards can also produce the same effect. Cellos and violas naturally produce low, tonal notes that are ideal. You can go online and find 432hz healing music on YouTube, or you can invest in cymbals and Tibetan bells in the right pitch.

At this point some people love to get very technical, and others prefer to go by instinct. Neither approach is wrong. If you roughly divide pitches into high, medium and low, and simply choose notes in the medium to low range, you will achieve much the same effect as someone who goes deeply into the technical aspect of music, frequency and so on. Our ancestors largely operated on instinct, and on observation.

Healing is associated with a higher frequency pitch, but if you only use that you are not addressing the current situation. The person starts off ill – lower pitch – and you are starting from a medium, neutral pitch, as the healer. So, you want to start out neutral, address the issue (low) and then create the reality you desire (high). Soothing music is also associated with healing, and that tends to be in the medium to low medium pitch.

If you have no other instrument to hand, use your voice. Humming, as discussed earlier, remains one of the

> most effective tools at your disposal – you can choose notes in advance or (and this is my personal preference) you can start with a medium pitch and work your way down four or five tones and back up again, then simply let inspiration (*Imbas*) take over. You may alternately hit higher notes for more healing energy and the odd lower note for emphasis or to tie the healing spell back to the root cause. You can experiment freely, both with your voice or an instrument.

I have not added words to this example, but we will look at that in the next chapter. Once you have a degree of confidence in constructing spells, using non-verbal Draíocht Ceoil, the rest will follow.

## Ending

Sometimes I continue the performance until I feel a natural end, but usually I will have a time frame in mind from the start. A spell is weakened by unnecessarily extending it. Again, it goes back to having a clear intent in mind. The time-consuming bit is the preparation, if done correctly. The performance does not need to be overly long. Once you have achieved a "crescendo" in the working, you're done.

In short, you need to create sound long enough in duration to express the intent, create the reality you desire and finally send the energy. This rarely exceeds ten minutes, and five is more usual for me. There are exceptions e.g. if you are creating wards and hexes to protect a space, or cleansing energy from a building, this can take several short performances over days, or one long performance. You will know once you have edited your working until it is as refined as possible – the length of time it takes to execute it, is the length of time you need.

If you set out your working in advance, decide how long it should last, and then commit to it – be truly present in the execution, give yourself over to it and focus seriously for that period – all will be well. Better a short, but well performed effort than a long, unequal one. However, we all have our own ways and if you feel a full-scale production complete with symphony orchestra is needed, go for it.

## Chapter 7

# Words and Draíocht Ceoil

Words are the final layer in our composition. We use them not only to add strength to the magic of sound but to refine our intent and aim our workings. If you ever want to understand the power of words, consider the simple three-word statement, "I love you," or its flip side, "I hate you," and the joy or devastation each can bring. We live to hear praise from those we respect, and we carry in our hearts the cruel or critical words that damage our self-esteem. My mother, who is 92, can recall in vivid detail a mean comment made by an aunt about her looks, as a child. A teacher can break a child's confidence with a handful of words. Equally, a kind word from a stranger can build confidence. There is an everyday kind of magic in our use of words, and when we become aware of this, we can employ them effectively.

In modern terms, we tend to divide poetry from music and talk in terms of the spoken versus the sung. Such differences are irrelevant in Draíocht Ceoil, which treats all sound as potentially powerful. However, music and words were traditionally divided into different "classes" and within each class, there was a hierarchy. In Draíocht Ceoil as we practice it today, these traditional separations are less important – we see each "class" as complementary and use each to create the whole. But it is interesting, and adds context, to understand how Old Irish society saw these divisions.

Similar to music, poetry was divided into three strains. These are *"Find"* (White, archaic form) *"Dubh"* (Black) and *"Breacc"* (Speckled) also called *"trefocal."*

Much of the work of the *Filí* was spread between these categories of poetry, and each is valuable in its own way.

*Find* or White referred to poetry of praise, eulogy, and positive reinforcement of the status of the individual or clan. While this can be dismissed by modern eyes as mere hagiography, it was far more than propaganda. *Find* poetry reinforced the good standing of notable figures. It was a reward for right action, a protection against calumny and satire. It lays claim to the land and political authority. This tapped into the belief among the Early Irish that if the *File* said it, it was true. Their words could literally call it into being. In modern Draíocht, it is seen as the origins of well-wishing others and providing healing, protection, and good luck.

*Dubh* or Black refers to poetry of censure, satire (*Áer*) and criticism while *Breacc,* to my mind the most interesting, refers to poems that mix praise and censure, and are considered to be warnings and predictions. *Dubh* satire was not spiteful. There were strictures against malicious or frivolous use of this very powerful tool. It provided a balance and check to the power of the elite, a reminder that honour was dependent on right action. *Filí* had the power to chastise, an early form of "speaking truth to power." It reminds us of our duty to speak up. It curbs the privilege of the powerful.

*Breacc,* or Speckled, is itself a word with many layers of meaning and is sometimes used to denote other words that have ambiguity. It is perhaps best described as the subtle and nuanced use of words. *Breacc* is also used to denote magic, prophesy, and messages from otherworldly entities. In Draíocht Ceoil, *Breacc* spells work well in situations where the source of trouble isn't clear, where you have to allow for other people's needs and where you hope to avoid outright conflict by making someone aware of their behaviour. You can create workings that allow for change, and redemption; you can acknowledge good and bad, and ensure that your judgment is fair.

In yet another way, *Breacc* can create a liminal moment, or words that are *Breacc* can be themselves, liminal – words that open the path between this reality and the next. While its origins are obviously in the Irish language, for those with limited access to Irish you can explore words in your own language that act in this way. There are words that will have nuanced significance for you, as an individual, that open you to the other realities or open you to inspiration.

*Breacc* is also used to refer to magic, in Irish traditions. Magic is not seen as white/dark, or good/bad – those dichotomies are modern constructs. Magic is a natural energy, and whether it results in good or evil depends on the practitioner. Moreover, it doesn't just depend on their intent, but on the skill with which they use it. You can have could intent but careless execution will lead to a bad result. *Breacc* is a way of acknowledging this and also that human motives and outlooks are subjective. We can try to be as objective as possible but there will always be an element of ambiguity.

If you meditate, spend time on contemplation of *Breacc*. Consider its various meanings. Try to identify words or phrases that can be taken in different ways, have different meanings.

Overall, be open to contemplation of all three categories of poetry, and you may be surprised by the links and associations that spring to mind.

### Filí and Musicians

The *Filí* are listed in the *Uraicecht Becc* as having seven degrees or levels, each with its own value and honour price. Poets, like harpists, were *"nemed"* – a term meaning something like sacred, noble or privileged – and *"saor"* meaning a free person in society. They were the repositories of lore, stories, genealogy and had supernatural powers. Poetic speech was used in law, in battle magic, in politics. Poets as a class were able to move freely from territory to territory and were often charged with diplomatic missions.

Sean O'Tuathail[38] wrote that above all other cultures and societies, ancient Ireland accorded poets a near divine rank, paying no taxes, and accorded a special place in law. (I wish I could persuade my family to accord me near divine status, but they just laugh when I suggest it!)

Poets as a class were allowed to traverse territorial boundaries and were entitled to the best accommodation and hospitality. To offend or harm one was to invite a poem of censure and could result in the loss of status and power. Hospitality was a duty in early Ireland and to neglect this was a serious breach of honour. Because society needed safe passage for the *Filí* between territories, any hint of disrespect had to be curbed.

In the *Bretha Nemed Déidenach,* a treatise on the power and privilege of poets, we are told that poets should be praised for their "ability to use language right on the edge of satire" – in Irish *"áor go ndath Molta 7 moladh go ndath náoire"* – and that the Poet's ability to use satire against those in power rendered them untouchable.

Indeed, the *Filí* ability to perform *Áer* (Satire). has heavily influenced the practice of *Draoí* throughout Irish culture. Satire in Early Irish society was a poetic expression used by the poets to rebuke authority. It took several forms, from curses to mockery and ridicule. If the satire landed justly, it had the power to bring out physical marks (three stripes, or boils) on the face of the individual. If used unjustly, punishment fell on the poet.

In a society where honour was the basis for status, satirists – sometimes called *Birach Bríathar*, or "Sharp with Words" – were greatly feared, especially female satirists who wielded a lot of power. There were strictures against the use of *Áer*, especially its improper use, with some texts calling it "un-poetry" but the ramifications if a satirist decided to ruin your reputation were immense.

Nowhere do we see more clearly the power of words, the employment of words and their esoteric meaning, as with the art of satire.

The File order's overall power in society cannot be underestimated: it lay in the respect accorded their rigorous training and the power they represented was that of *Firenne,* or Truth. This is what rendered satire so important. Furthermore, as a class they claimed divine lineage – from *"Brian and Iuchar and Úar, the sons of Bress son of Eladan and Brigit the woman-poet, daughter of the Great Dagda"* (Book of Leinster). It persisted well into Christian medieval Ireland: in both the *Seanchas Már* and the *Bretha Nemed,* St Patrick renewed the power of *Filí* to enact judgments across territorial lines and borders: even into enemy territory. Their position as "outside" society was at the heart of their ability to speak up to chieftains, and ignore the usual rules of allegiance, something that is reflected in folklore in late medieval and modern Ireland. The wise woman occupies a similar position, being both an integral part of her community and simultaneously, being able to move outside the normal rules.

Scholars debate whether they "sang" and dispute the level of separation between poets, who operated through spoken words, and musicians: we know that the lower grade of poet was a bard, but that they were distinct from the order of *Oirfideadh,* or musicians. The word "bard" has entered our modern language as a catch all for any "Celtic" musician, which confuses people but for the purposes of accuracy we will use the terms in their correct meaning – *Filí, Bard* and *Oirfideadh.* The bard is more a musician-accompanist to the poet. The *Oirfideadh* is a Master of Music, and usually a harpist.

While scholars debate the nuances of each group's rights and privileges, what becomes clear to any student of old and medieval Irish poetry is that they are united by a solid belief in the power of sound, both verbal and instrumental. It also becomes clear that each enjoys to some degree the power to act as an intermediary or conduit between the Otherworld and this reality. To take one example, a member of the higher degree of poets can perform prophetic poetry, and deliver judgment inspired by *Imbas* (inspiration). The Harpist is given a similar status, the ability to deliver music that channels magic or provides messages from the supernatural.

The most skilled and respected of the poets and musicians had access to power – they were respected by the elite classes and allowed to move among them. Just as the poet could deliver judgment on a Chieftain, and wield a degree of political power, the Master Harper (*Sui Cruitirechta*) was a fixture at every elite social occasion, and a reflection of the status and power of their patron. Honour and reputation could be harmed by any disrespect shown to the Harpist.

It is important to remember that this special status survived into the Christian era: there was a similar elevation of music among the Monastery orders, especially Psalm Singers. The patronage of the Chieftain was integral to the survival of the *Filí* as an order, into relatively modern times. The lines between Poet, *Bard* and Musician blur more and more as time progresses, and the calamity that was the Cromwellian era in Ireland reduced much of the old order to remnants, struggling to survive. This is when much of the established practice passes into folk lore, and folk magic.

In modern times, the respect accorded to poetry and written word continues – the influence of poets on the revolutionary movement of the 19th and 20th century cannot be overstated, and our fledgling nation was shaped and viewed through the lens of both sympathetic and critical writing. Much of our national identity has been shaped by the imagining and re-imagining of Irishness by both native and Ascendancy (Anglo-Irish) writers. Their words helped to birth a nation and launch a rebellion against an Empire.

## Poetry, Lyrics and Music

Irish culture has always emphasized a complex synergy between music, and words: together, both are greater than the sum of their parts. We can create mood, convey messages that are not only overt but covert, manipulate emotion, by combining the two. A very Irish example of this is the genre of Rebel Songs. From the haunting strains of *Boolavogue,* to rousing tunes such as *A Nation Once Again,* the history of rebellion can be traced, which had a very real effect on the attitudes and beliefs of a nation. As with poetry and literature, songs helped create the image of nationhood in the Irish psyche.

We see the same in modern music. "Fight music" uses insistent rhythm, crescendos, thrilling musical passages combined with stirring lyrics to induce a sense of urgency, bravery, determination in the audience. Love songs use pathos, both in music and lyrics, to induce empathy or use uplifting phrases of composition combined with passionate lyrics to create romance. Differentiation between poetry and lyrics becomes redundant at this point – both poetry and lyrics can, when powerful enough, provoke a response that is similar. It is both intellectual and emotional, and it speaks to us of a communal human experience.

The *Filí* understood the power of performance, and the effect of combining words and music as did their Christian descendants. The great corpus of religious music from early church through to Baroque exalted the human spirit and produced religious and spiritual ecstasy.

When we compose a spell using Draíocht Ceoil, it has much in common with ballads or modern songs – we use music and lyrics together to convey our intent, and we are constrained by space to fit in as much as possible, as meaningfully as possible, into a short form. The need to fit in a great deal into a short burst of music and words creates a tension that, if used properly, adds urgency to our workings. Poetry is, in my own words, the art of saying as much as possible in as few words as possible. To achieve this, we convey deeper meanings and in the tradition of the *Filí*, many layers of meaning, using metaphor and imagery. Adding this to music results in a potent and dynamic recipe.

## The Language of the Filí

The poets had a special language, a learned code where each word had multiple meanings and the ability to turn a phrase neatly using these many interpretations of a word was highly prized. While much of this is lost to us now, we see examples of it in legal tracts and primers, and understanding the concept of multi-layered meanings is vital to Draíocht Ceoil.

In the Rosc, the poetic form used for all kinds of public duties including battle magic, legal judgments, and political arguments, the use of words that can be turned to mean several things reflects both the skill of the poet, and the erudition of the audience. The poet demonstrates their expertise by their choice of words, and the learned, elite listener shows their superiority by understanding and appreciating all the possible interpretations.

In Draíocht Ceoil, using a single word, with many meanings, some of which may be highly obscure adds a depth of power to magical workings, and was the root of poetic status. In legal matters, the use of poetic language was vital, and in this context "poetic" was understood to mean deeply layered words, given in one of the many recognized Irish poetic forms, which taken all together rendered proper judgments. Rosc poetry was the most important poetic form for legal exposition as well as for political and magical tracts.

In an oral tradition, such as Old Irish society, the importance of sound and spoken word is far greater than in a written tradition. Imagine reading the words of a rap song on paper, compared to hearing them spoken with the emphasis, stress patterns, rhythmic rhyming patterns and delivery of the artist... on paper what looks like doggerel transforms into meaningful, energetic poetry in the moment of delivery. This is the difference between reading poetry and literature from the early period, and the way in which they would have been performed at the time.

Performance cannot be over emphasized, and by performance, I mean not only the outward delivery but the individual spin each poet puts on the conventional form.

When your qualification as a scholar, lawyer or political advisor depends on the body of knowledge contained in your head, and every other qualified person contains the same knowledge, your ability to transform that knowledge into living, impactful action – especially through the poetic forms such as the Rosc – is what sets you apart. The poet was judged on their ability to render an "extemporaneous" verse – a verse composed on the spot. In practice this meant the poet would consider all the factors before them, political or legal, draw on their extensive repertoire of memorized forms, examples, precedents and poetry, but in the moment of delivery, open themselves to "*Imbas*" i.e. inspiration.

This moment of *Imbas* was the difference between dryly recounting memorized forms – and delivering something that would be deemed wisdom. The poets who reached the highest status were those who demonstrated this.

## The Use of Words in Folk Magic

There are several forms of Draíocht Ceoil in which words are especially important, as seen in the folk practices of the last few hundred years. Some involve purely extemporaneous compositions, and some involve reusing existing songs, putting new words to existing music but in each case, or composing pieces in advance. Obviously, these lines can become blurred, and in every pre-composed work there should be room for inspiration but we can roughly divide them into "Extemporaneous," and "Composed." We can also loosely ascribe *Brí* or *Bua* energy to each example.

Examples include:

- Extemporaneous chanting *(Brí)* including Lilting: used while doing repetitive tasks like spinning or churning, in moments of *Imbas*, or while meditating.
- Keening (*Bua*): Laments for the dead, facilitating grieving (extemporaneous, in its original form at least, but conforms to established poetic conventions).
- *Gleann Diceann* – "The Hard Word" a form of cursing (*Bua/Brí*) usually composed in advance but can also be spur of the moment. (See Chapter 13).
- Lullabies – used to fend off changelings, to protect babies (*Bua*) (Composed).
- Love songs, Healing songs (*Brí/Bua*) (composed)
- Agricultural and Labouring Songs designed to help sowing/harvesting/milking (*Brí*) (composed but tied to nature, outdoor activities, designed to attune to the natural world).

I have marked them generally as either extemporaneous or composed, but it is important to remember that most are in practice a mixture of both. Just as the poet would practice and commit to memory the forms and precedents of a topic but rely on a moment of *Imbas* to create the actual delivery, the practitioner of Draíocht Ceoil will construct a spell with care but remain open to inspiration in the moment of performing it. Becoming open in this way is a matter of practice, allowing the words and sound to come through without conscious choice.

Similarly, while it is interesting to note their *Brí* or *Bua* energy, in practice there will always be an element of both at play. Trusting your instincts becomes more and more important at this stage rather than trying to laboriously conform to a rigid template. Go with your gut.

## Extemporaneous Chanting

As mentioned before, spells are constructed using sound, primarily musical notes or non-verbal sound, and then overlaid with words – ones of inherent power and meaning, or non-lexical "nonsense" sounds with the same. Again, extemporaneous chanting is the way to unlock these non-lexical sounds, practicing them, and understanding their use.

Traditionally, in folk magic, repetitive tasks such as spinning and churning were heavily associated with extemporaneous chanting. Any task that engages your hands but leaves your mind free to wander is ideal. You can sing, or even hum, to get started then allow yourself to make words or word-like sounds. If you've ever heard folk songs with lyrics such as "tiddledeeeye" or "foll loll loll" you've heard non-lexical or "nonsense" words. Listen to Whiskey in the Jar (personally I love the Thin Lizzy version) and you'll hear the lyrics:

*"Mush-a ring dumb-a do dumb-a da*
*Whack fall the daddy-o, whack fall the daddy-o"*

These are a combination of words mutated from Gaeilge and nonsense words. These are evocative sounds, which suit the rousing, rebellious nature of the song. They also hold the beat, the stresses and emphasis, of the tune.

In Draíocht Ceoil, when creating a spell, it is often easiest to take a well-known tune, add words and use it for your working. Start by adding nonsense words. Don't worry about meanings, just use sounds to suit the tune. Alternate between fast and slow tunes, and between emotions. Because of the "wild" or unconscious aspect of this practice, it is held to have *Brí* energy. Nonsense words contain sounds that are considered inherently powerful including High, Medium and Low resonances.

Lilting, *portaireacht bhéil* (mouth music) in Irish traditional music is closely related to chanting. Lilting is designed to imitate the patterns of certain instruments, notably the harp. It follows the stresses that create the unique rhythms of Irish music, "singing melodies on improvised nonsense syllables, often in an attempt to imitate an instrumental sound."[39]

Lilters used sounds that also mimic the internal rhyming of Irish poetic forms e.g.:

*"Tee—ow-dle di-dl-dee dum, die-dle i-dl-i die-dle ee-di-um"*
(Josie McDermott, Collier's Reel)

When lilting to an instrument, certain vowels and consonants present themselves more naturally than others – giving the example of fiddle playing, with soft "s" representing bow changes and long vowels such as aye, ay, eee, in the held notes. Specific sounds – certain vowels and consonants – are associated with Lilting in general and in turn certain tunes have their own traditional set of lilts. The practice itself had overtones of magical music, of Sidhe music and the recording of tunes overheard in forts and duns.

Historically, the practice of lilting was born from a need to memorize tunes and preserve them (especially from the Cromwellian era onward) and became a way of providing music when musicians were in short supply. This was primarily a female task by the early twentieth century and many of our now famous tunes were learned by musicians from women who had carried them "in their heads."[40] In modern Irish slang we use *"tiddledeeeye"* to mean Irish folk music, lilting, and *sean nós* singing.

Lilting also teaches ornamentation and grace notes, hugely important to both Irish music and Draíocht Ceoil. Like nonsense words, grace notes are a way to create unique variants on a familiar tune. It falls into extemporaneous and *Imbas* based creation of sound energy as well as the spontaneous creation of music, Sean Nós style but with the structure we associate with other forms. It encourages the creation of sound energy within a traditional convention. As with the exercise for Extemporizing, lilting or humming is a perfect exercise to open yourself to *Imbas*.

## Keening

I will address Keening in Chapter 9 but in short, it is the practice of composing extemporaneous laments for the dead, a tradition that survived into the early 20th century. It is a public performance, tied to the status and reputation of the individual, and providing a bridge between the living and the dead. It helped to regulate expressions of grief, as well as facilitate them, it also curtailed excessive demonstrations of the same. In Draíocht Ceoil as in the wider community, it has become difficult to recreate anything approaching the original traditions of keening. What few recordings that remain to us are mere echoes of remembered laments, and accounts of keening were filtered through critical eyes – disapproving church members, Ascendancy and British commentators, and patronizing academics.

However, with the rise in people seeking traditional burial rites, there is some resurgence of interest that has led to a form of keening, albeit a reconstructed and re-imagined form, to help with grief and facilitate the passing of souls.

As a magical tool, the concept can be used to mourn or put to rest old relationships and past trauma. The words used in Keening are both "nonsense words," and words of praise and loss. I have written and performed ceremonies to mark the end of marriages or relationships, use the Keening tradition of both praising and grieving. No matter how bad a relationship was, it is important to acknowledge the joy it once brought, even potentially. It is important to praise anything good that came from it, – for example, children, or friends, or a home. When the person is ready to praise and mourn honestly, they are ready to start moving on. Draíocht Ceoil can help to nurture this, mark it, and then magically protect it going forward.

## Gleann Diceann

In Old Irish poetry, the *Gleann Diceann* was the form of satire known as the "endless bite" and in Chapter 13 we will look at its history in relation to Hexing. It was one of the forms of satire used by the *Filí,* but it is used in a wider sense in Draíocht Ceoil, often called "The Hard Word." This can be to "put the hard word on someone," meaning to hex them – the implication being to give them a taste of their own medicine or "to speak the hard word," meaning to name and shame, or expose the truth of what someone is doing.

The *Gleann Diceann* was feared because it held the unmistakable ring of truth. In folk magic, invoking "the hard word" without just cause was taboo. It always had an element of public interest to it, rather than domestic. It was reserved for people or causes that affected the community at large. A curse against a landlord would be a *Gleann Diceann,* whereas a curse against a neighbour over a personal dispute would not. However, if the neighbour publicly slandered you, this becomes a community issue, threatening your status and the peace of the community. Then, the Hard Word becomes appropriate.

It was also associated with speaking truth, bearing witness, or giving testimony to others. For example, if the cause of a problem was in dispute, the *Gleann Diceann* was invoked to either pressure people to tell the truth and reveal the culprit or to reveal the culprit directly, and in both cases, by magical means. Spells that reveal the true intent of individuals or reveal the source of ill-wishing are under this practice. Words used in *Gleann Diceann* tend to be confrontational, accusing, revealing.

## Love Songs and Love Magic

Sometimes love spells are treated as silly or inappropriate. The truth is that historically, love spells were hugely important in Irish folk magic and Draíocht Ceoil in particular utilized love songs, from at least Norman times onward.[41]

Love as a concept is not as straightforward as our modern sensibilities might suggest. The ideas of courtly love and romantic love have a complex relationship with the business of marriage and all three are tied up with the status of women in medieval and modern Ireland. For the average Irish woman, marriage was almost the only way to secure one's future, a situation that existed until the latter half of the twentieth century. With few protections afforded in law, and with access to legal processes denied to the Irish population for several generations, the harsh reality for women was that money, land and education were in the hands of men. Your choices involved marriage (with at least the chance of a household, children and respectable status) or a convent (a lifetime of enforced chastity but some status in the community) or a lifetime of drudgery. Before the famine, parents tried to provide for their children equally. After the famine, the practice of subdividing land stopped, and it became common to leave the land to the eldest male. While this solved the problems caused by fragmentation of holdings into parcels unable to support a family, it left younger siblings in a precarious situation, dependent on the charity of the eldest son.

For men, this meant being a labourer on the family farm, sometimes dependent on their brother and sister-in-law for a small stipend. However, there was always the option of employment elsewhere, travelling or emigrating for work, and greater scope for independence. For women, there were fewer opportunities, and they often became unpaid skivvies in their brother's home and if he married, they could be turned out or demoted even further to the status of maids under the control of their sisters-in-law. Without a dowry, their prospects of marriage were slim. If their family was of the labouring class rather than small-holding or farming class, they were in a very insecure position indeed.

Love spells exist in this cultural context as expressions of genuine need. People were not trying to get a boyfriend, they were trying to secure a future and as with any branch of folk magic, necessity was a powerful force. Women weaved spells not only for themselves but for female friends and family; they also approached the *Bean Feasa* for help in attracting a suitor. Sometimes there was a specific individual targeted, and sometimes it was a general call to the universe to provide an interested party. Both were considered normal and moral. The aim wasn't to trap the person against their will, but rather to entice their eye to the virtues of the potential wife.

Over mundane tasks such as churning and spinning, women sang songs about the type of suitor they envisaged, hoping to call them forward by sheer force of will. They also sang and chanted while baking and offered the resulting bread or cake to the object of their affection. They used extemporaneous composition as well as established love songs and poems. Because it pertains to the human institution of marriage, love magic is considered to have mainly *Bua* energy. Words used in Love magic tend to be soothing, caressing, loving, and romantic.

## Lullabies

Not only were lullabies used to soothe babies, in Draíocht Ceoil they were used to protect babies from the attention of the Sidhe. Lullabies are still used to create safe spaces and are a mix of non-lexical sounds and crooning, with words that express love, safety, care. Also worth noting is that some traditional lullabies create dissonance between the soothing lullaby and the words. *Rock-a-bye Baby,* for example, with its "and down will come baby and cradle and all." You can explore the effect of using dissonance in your workings in a similar way.

## Working Songs

An interesting point is that because the practice of singing while labouring was largely extemporaneous, few Irish examples have survived into the modern era. This has led some commentators to assert the practice was uncommon, but we know from various sources that people did sing to relieve the tedium. Like Keening, the highly individual and transient nature of the song meant that they were not of a nature to be recorded.

Examples of surviving working songs include one entitled "*Amhrán na Cuiginne*" (trad), in which a woman churning the milk sings about the boy she loves, who is the cow herder. Edward Bunting collected instrumental pieces known as "The Spinning Wheel Songs," annotated as "very ancient, author and date unknown." The more famous *Spinning Wheel Song (Ballad)* has lyrics that mimic the whirr and turn of the wheel, while telling a story of a maiden sneaking out to meet a lover under the nose of her dozing Grandmother.

*"Mellow the moonlight to shine is beginning*
*Close by the window young Eileen is spinning*
*Bent o'er the fire her blind grandmother sitting*
*Crooning and moaning and drowsily knitting.*
*Merrily cheerily noiselessly whirring Spins the wheel,*
*rings the wheel while the foot's stirring*
*Sprightly and lightly and merrily ringing*
*Sounds the sweet voice of the young maiden singing."*
(trad).

The lyrics are notable for their double reference to singing while working, as we see the old lady "crooning" over her knitting, even as the young maid sings her into drowsiness while spinning.

One type of working song that did survive to be recorded is the Sea Shanty, songs used on board ships to help morale and synchronize labour. Different types of shanties suited different tasks e.g. the Capstan shanty was ideal for raising or lowering the anchor among other jobs. Other forms were the Pump and Halyard, but songs could be adjusted to suit each task. The pace and structure changed to suit the needs of the deckhands, and the "shanty man" was responsible for setting the pace and leading the song. Sea Shanties borrow from several different cultures, but the Irish influence is heavy. The famous *What shall we do with the drunken sailor*, is, of course, the same melody as the Irish song *"Oró sé do beatha 'bhaile."*

As you can see, both nonsense words and words that mimic the rhythm of the work are used in working songs. In Draíocht Ceoil, they imbue work with good luck or magic. For example, when spinning the singer might imbue the yarn with good luck or use the opportunity to sing about a desired lover.

## Choosing Words Wisely

Whether sung or spoken, words are part of the magic of sound. While nonsense words and extemporaneous chanting are important, knowing how to compose creative but effective spells involves more than that. Every word is important, and understanding their layers of meaning, and how to choose them, is the key to effective workings.

As mentioned in Chapter 1, the first choice is between Irish and English – a choice fraught with historical and political significance. The history of the Irish language is both rich and tragic. Over the eight hundred years of occupation and oppression, the Irish language was the target of colonial ire. Destroying our culture started with destroying our language.

There were languages that predated Gaeilge in Ireland, but at least 2,500 years ago it became the common language, spreading out to Scotland, The Isle of Man and further afield. By the era of Christianization, it was the established language and neither the introduction of Latin, nor Viking settlement, could derail it. We see some loan words entering the language, *Pingín* for penny, *Margadh* for market, but the Gaelic culture remains untroubled. The prevalence of manuscripts from this era displays its strength.

The next threat to Irish as a language and culture came from the Normans but while they introduced a period of bilingualism, in the end Irish won out. Even the Norman lords began to speak Irish and adopt Irish customs, leading to the popular phrase calling them, "more Irish than the Irish themselves." Anglo-Norman words such as garcon (boy) became *Garsún*, a word that survives into both Gaeilge and Hiberno-English today.

The real legacy of the Norman invasion and subsequent events was to eventually make English rather than Irish the administrative language. Irish remained the poetic and literary language, as well as the commonly spoken tongue but was removed from political power. Article III of The Statute of Kilkenny 1367 made it illegal for English colonists to speak Irish and for the native Irish to speak their language when interacting with the colonists. This is reinforced in 1537 with The Statute of Ireland – An Act for the English Order Habit and Language and The Administration of Justice (Language) Act (Ireland) 1737 which together not only made it illegal to use Irish in a court or in legal transactions, but imposed hefty fines for speaking it inside a courtroom. This effectively removed justice from the grasp of any native Irish speaker and made adopting English a matter of necessity.

However, until the famine, almost 40% of the population spoke fluent Irish, despite these strictures. After the Famine the numbers dwindled rapidly, especially as the worst hit areas coincided with the Gaeltacht (Irish speaking) areas. Being a primarily Irish speaking person was dangerous, as evidenced by the Maamtrasna Murder Trial in 1882, where the Irish speaking defendants could not get a fair trial, and even their solicitor did not speak Irish. This resulted in the hanging of an innocent man.[42]

It is mainly in the period 1600 to 1900 that we see the both systematic oppression of the Irish identity, and the pressure to adopt English as a language, and anglicized culture, for economic and political survival.

The Gaelic Revival of the late 19th and early 20th centuries restored and reinvented a sense of national pride and identity, starting with the cultivation and elevation of the Irish language. This period sees tension between the native Irish and the Anglo-Irish, known as The Ascendancy, whose interest in Irish culture was filtered through their own prejudices and agenda. To this day, many read Lady Gregory's interpretation of Irish myths without realizing the damage she did in "civilizing" our literature. Similarly, I wince when people consider Yeats the epitome of Irish poetry, ignoring writers like Kinsella, Clarke or Kavanagh. This is not a failure unique to the Ascendancy -after all the very monks who recorded the pre-Christian stories, thus preserving them, were not above commentating and editing. One such scribe wrote in the margins of the *Táin Bó Cualnge* that "some things were the work of the devil, some are poetic inventions, some are true, and some are meant for the delight of fools."[43] However, the influence of the Anglo-Irish class on popular understanding of indigenous Irish culture is an ever present issue.

The attempts to revive Irish as a language were sometimes treated as secondary and quixotic by this class, while it became more widespread throughout the working-class Irish especially in Urban areas. In the 1901 census James Monahan, my great grandfather, living in Stephen Street Lower, Dublin 2, lists his family as monolingual-English speaking. By 1911, they are proud bilinguists and all the children list Irish and English as their spoken language. In the 1930s, my father was reared on the Northside of Dublin and spoke only Irish until he was ten years of age. This was not an uncommon thing, as pride in Irish created a revival in the Dublin Irish dialect. But English continued to dominate public life while through the efforts of organizations like the Gaelic League, the Gaelic Athletic Association (Cumann

Lúthchleas Gael) and the Ossianic Society, Irish was restored to a position of respect within the education, culture and politics.

Its fate under the new Irish state has been mixed. It is a mandatory language in schools, but much criticism is leveled at how it is taught and how few people speak it in daily life. On the other hand, year on year the number of Irish adults studying Irish and trying to speak it has increased, many learning conversational Irish through Gael Linn or indeed on modern language apps. 39.8% of Irish adults lay claim to some proficiency in Irish, according to the 2022 census. On the 13th of June 2005, Irish became an official language of the European Union. All official documents and information from the Irish state must be provided in both English and Irish, restoring Irish to some degree as an administrative language.

Irish as a language is the soul of our culture, and while learning to speak it fluently may not be feasible for everyone, learning a few words is certainly achievable. We often exhort each other in Ireland to use the *"cúpla focail"* – the few words we have, even if the grammar isn't correct or we need to add in English words to complete the thought. For readers outside Ireland, who find the idea of learning a language daunting, there are words that are very useful in creating Draíocht Ceoil (see list below). But what anyone can do is seek out Irish language programmes, videos or music, and just listen. Listen to the rhythm and "lilt" of the language. Absorb the overall sound of Irish as a language and store it away.

Similarly, I would say listen to Hiberno-English. This is the unique form of English spoken in Ireland, and again for those outside the culture, it sounds nothing like the "Stage Oirish" you'll hear in American films, or in TV shows. Seek out Irish broadcasters such as RTE, watch modern Irish films and listen to modern Irish music. What makes Hiberno-English unique is its blending of Irish syntax and form with the English language. Immersing yourself in both the sound and the information about Ireland will benefit you. Read both classic and modern Irish writers. I wouldn't inflict *Ulysses* on anyone, but James Joyce's short story *The Dead* is extraordinary. Read a little Flann O'Brien, and Brendan Behan. But also read Sally Rooney, Marian Keyes, Colm Tobin, and Donal Ryan.

In practice, many of the folk practices of the last few hundred years would have been carried out in English, or more accurately a mixture of inherited Irish words mixed with Hiberno-English. While the National Schools Collection reflects a certain amount of folklore passed on in Irish, the reality is by the nineteenth century a large proportion of the population conducted their everyday life in English. There is nothing wrong or inauthentic in following suit.

## The Irish Poetic Forms

There are many set poetic forms used in Old Irish literature, and each has their own very specific set of rules. Taking just one example, the *Ae Freislighe,* this form requires four-line verses, each first and third containing three-syllable words, and rhyming with each other while the second and fourth lines have two syllable words. The same word opens and closes the verse – a technique called "*Dúnadh*" (closing).

Each is similarly complex, including *Seadna,* (alternating lines of eight and seven syllables) or *Dechnad Mor,* which includes alliteration, internal rhymes, and end rhymes. While it is interesting to learn more about them, none of them survived intact into the folk practice of Draíocht Ceoil, but we did inherit echoes of these complicated literary forms especially internal rhymes, rhythms and so on.

In the case of the Rosc, arguably the most important of the poetic forms, we know quite a lot about the rules and how they add power to the composition. But by examining the rules of any of these forms we can get inspiration. However, if you prefer not to use these older forms, and compose in your own style, which is fine. I personally feel that incorporating some of the tricks of the older poetic forms into compositions helps to root your work in the Irish culture, and gives you tools ideally suited to Draíocht Ceoil.

In the next chapter we will look more closely at the Rosc, and its importance in Irish magic, hopefully giving you the basic tools needed to use it in your own workings.

The use of Irish poetic forms survived into the modern era. One example from the 18th century is the poet Piaras Mac Gearailt – his body of work includes 45 poems, some of them Rosc form, mainly Jacobite in politics. One, the *Battle Cry of Munster*, invokes the fighting spirit of the Irish and became not only an anthem of his day but a rebel song for modern times. The Irish group, The Wolf Tones, recorded their version as did many other groups and singers.

## Non-Lexical Words

A lot of the power of nonsense words comes from the inherent power of certain sounds. In particular, varying between long and short vowel sounds and the use of specific consonants to break up these sounds, is what creates power, and the use of rhythm and stressed notes, adds urgency. Picking words of power and then framing them between powerful non-lexical sounds adds depth to your working and layers of meaning.

If you consider the vowel sounds "ah/ay" and "eye/eee" and take the breathy sound of "beh/bee" and "deh/dee" you can combine in various ways: dee-eh, bee-ay, beh-ah, deh-ay. Bee-eh, bee-eye Another satisfying sound is "um" or "umb"

*dee-ay, bee-eye, beh-eee, dee-umb, dee-um bee-eye, beh-eee*

You can experiment and practice with any combination of stress and sound, and you can both build up a "go-to" list of nonsense words that work for you as well as just winging it. If you want, you can go one layer further, and link your "nonsense" sounds to Ogham, choosing them both for their inherent sound values and their meaning in the various Ogham kennings.

## Ogham and Nonsense Words

A basic understanding of Ogham will be useful: to this end, I highly recommend The Ogham Academy and the Irish Pagan School. What I offer here is a very brief and simple overview to explain this one use of it in Draíocht Ceoil.

Ogham is an early medieval Irish system of writing, comprised of parallel strokes across or to the side of a continuous line. Examples found on stones around Ireland are mainly boundary markers, and markers for heroic or powerful figures. By the late 14th century, it had become a system of writing that linked various attributes to each letter, there being three known lists of *Bríatharogam* or Word-ogham. From texts like the In *Lebor Ogaim* and the *Book of Ballymote*, there is a body of work that provides meanings for each of the "letters" of the Ogham. The word ogham really refers to the form of letters or script, while the letters are more properly known collectively as the Beith-luis-nin after the letter names of the first letters. Each character is called a feda.

The text In *Lebor Ogaim* lists many different glosses for each fid, or letter. The tree glosses are the ones that have been popularized in modern Neopaganism, but the *Filí* were said to have over 150 variants memorized.[44] Modern writers such as Robert Graves plundered Ogham to create their own systems, including the notorious Celtic Tree Calendar and other modern inventions. This is why pursuing accurate information about Ogham is imperative: there is an unfortunate amount of nonsense out there. But it is worth the effort: exploring Ogham meanings and choosing sounds accordingly can add more depth to your working.

When you have decided on a word of power, and are constructing your working, writing it in Ogham can reinforce that power. Similarly, you can create a ward using Ogham letters, or you can inscribe Ogham on a candle used in a working. Simple but effective ways to root your practice in Irish culture.

## Useful Words as Gaeilge

*Healing*
Health – *Sláinte*
Illness – *Tinneas*
Disease – Galar

*Luck*
Luck- Adh
Bad luck – *Droch-adh*
Misfortune – *Mí-adh*

*Friendship*
Friend – *Cara, Mo Chara* (my friend)
Friendship – *Cairdeas*

*Boundary*
Boundary – Teorainn
Welcome – Fáilte
Protection – Consaint

*Miscellaneous*
Lies – Bréága
Deception -Mheabhlaireacht

## Chapter 8

# The Rosc

The Rosc, used in everything from Battle Magic to Law, is a fascinating area of study by itself. My class at the Irish Pagan School covers the Rosc in detail, but for the purposes of this book, here is a short overview.

There are several elements that the Rosc must contain, and almost all examples of the art conform to these. Modern versions sometimes vary in tense or omit the *Dúnadh,* but they need to hit most of the following points to be considered Rosc.

**Freeform**: A Rosc is not metrical nor do the lines rhyme. It more closely resembles modern freeform poetry than anything.

**Rhythm/Lilt**: Rosc poetry relies on alliteration and internal rhymes, a feature of poetry in Irish and Hiberno-English right up to the present day. The use of clear stress patterns adds urgency and emphasis.

**Spoken/Public**: The Rosc is reserved for important public issues and should have an element of public performance. Originally, it would have been performed as Battle Magic, in the presence of the troops, and also perhaps the enemy forces; as legal arguments or judgments, in the presence of those concerned in the case, the royal court, or the political assembly.

While drawing heavily on a body of memorized literature, a Rosc should be performed in the "Extemporaneous" manner. While there are agreed conventions and structure, and in the case of legal arguments, it is reasonable to accept that the basic shape of them would have been prepared in advance, the final composition must be shaped by *Imbas* (inspiration), and its delivery is highly stylized. It uses vivid imagery and metaphor rather than explicit description, conveying complex emotional and philosophical ideas through deceptively simple lines.

Reiteration including the repetition of key words and phrases, opening and closing lines reflecting each other, and reiteration of emphasis, is used to add emphasis and stress the key points of the poem.

Rosc poems are often "locked" (*Dúnadh*) by ending on the same phrase as the beginning. They are used to deliver both individual monologues, and back and forth exchanges in a magical battle of wits. This technique of *Dúnadh* is also a powerful magical tool, completing the spell within its own circle and preventing mishaps when delivered.

Its delivery was public. The prestige of the file depended on the attentive interest of the prestige classes and the puns and linguistic complexity appealed especially to them. However, tales of battle magic and the heroic cycles all featured Rosc poetry, and were performed for general enjoyment, implying that people of the time were at least partially familiar with the nuances of poetic language.

Various sources including *Bretha Nemed* and *Sanas Cormaic* detail the performance of the Rosc as accompanied by music, actions, drama. On the written page, it already stands out from texts by its alliterative, non-metrical style and stress patterns, and similarly during any public recitation, these unique traits marked it out as indicating moments of heightened emotion.

The delivery of the Rosc was described as accompanied by symbolic, magical gestures or positions, for example, standing on one leg, one arm behind the back, one eye closed. This is the *corrguineacht* usually translated as "crane pose."

Two famous Old Irish law tracts – *Uraicecht Becc* and *Bretha Nemed Toísech* – not only hold up the Rosc as a "rock of the law," but are themselves written in poetic language, with the latter largely written in Rosc form. They both state that it is vitally important that the Rosc be composed by someone fit for the job, a master of language and understanding of the law.

However, the *Bretha Nemed* goes even further and states they must also have a wider understanding of justice:

> *"Problems are more numerous than the canon law; obscurities are more numerous than what is laid down in the law."*

In other words, one must understand more than the mere letter of the law. It goes on to add:

> *"Prolific nature can undermine the suit it is neither Roscad nor chanting that apportions truth to all."*

This means, that neither learning off the rules of the Rosc (Roscad, the Old Irish plural) nor the ability to chant one off by rote, will bring forth Firenne, Truth. These texts clearly link Rosc to inspiration, and foras i.e., the moment of action and the principles on which that action is based. The principles are the years of learning, and the body of knowledge stored in the poet's head, the action is the creation of a new, truthful judgment in the moment. This is part of the characteristics of a Rosc, to create extemporaneous, inspired, composition rather than learning by rote.

There are several very famous Rosc poems in Early Irish literature. One example is from the *Cath Maige Tuiread* (Battle of Moytura) (translation Grey, 1982)[45]

*Kings arise to [meet] the battle*
*Cheeks are seized*
*Faces [honours] are declared*

*Flesh is decimated,*
*Faces are flayed*
*[?]of battle are seized*
*Ramparts are sought*
*Feasts are given*
*Battles are observed*
*Poems are recited*
*Druids are celebrated*
*Circuits are made*
*Bodies are recorded*
*Metals cut*
*Teeth mark*
*Necks break*
*A hundred cuts blossom*
*Screams are heard*
*Battalions are broken*
*Hosts give battle*
*Ships are steered*
*Weapons protect*
*Noses are severed*
*I see all who are born*
*in blood-zealous vigorous battle,*
*raging [on the] raven-battlefield [with] blade-scabbards.*
*They attempt our defeat*
*over our own great torrents*
*Against your attack on the full [compliment] of Fomoire*
*In the mossy margins;*
*the helpful raven drives*
*strife to our hardy hosts*
*mustered, we prepare ourselves to destroy*
*To me, the full-blooded exploits are like*
*shaking to-and-fro of hound-kills*
*goodly decay of muddy war-bands, your violations are renounced.*

The entire poem reads as if they are commenting on the battle, but it is in fact a prophecy of how the battle will unfold. Or perhaps to take it a step further, it is a statement of will – this is what I want to happen, therefore it will come to pass.

Learning to compose Rosc poetry is a valuable exercise for anyone interested in Irish Draíocht, not just Draíocht Ceoil but it is very important for the latter. Rosc poetry requires practice – both to master the form, with its traditional Irish poetic conventions and to master the art of *Imbas* Forosnai. There are several things you can do to help yourself along, and the first is to explore the concept of extemporaneous verse as mentioned above. Opening yourself to inspiration and allowing words, thoughts, poetry to form without consciously shaping them, is a solid way to start. It is something you can practice anywhere, at any idle moment, and you may be surprised to see what comes to you.

## Survival into Modern Times

Storytelling until recent times was carried out through a variety of performances, including poetry, verse, prose, ballads, opera, dance and ballet. Words and music combined created systems of knowledge that convey social norms and cultural beliefs. While it would be an exaggeration to claim the Rosc itself survived in common usage, it is not a stretch by any means to point to the traditions of public and private entertainment in Ireland up to this century and see the parallels with older traditions.

In recent years, I and others have used the Rosc form in public workings: I run a small Facebook group called Draíocht Ceoil and The Rosc, which you are welcome to join to get help in writing Rosc. I also have a class at the Irish Pagan School on the subject. You will also find several invaluable texts on the Rosc online.

I offer here a Rosc I wrote several years ago, which was performed by several groups in Ireland and which was subsequently published in *Gods and Radicals Magazine*: the occasion was the proposed visit from a misogynistic American to Ireland, a man who called himself a "King" and who was calling on Irish men to attend a rally decrying Irish women for being...well, superior. I did not like this proposal. Nor did many Irish people, of all genders. As a contribution to the cause, I offered this as a Rosc, to be used as people saw fit, and they did so to great effect. (Spoiler – the "king" called off his visit, citing fear of Irish women as the reason. Oh, how we laughed.

Note the way the Rosc is embedded in a few lines of prose, a sample of which is given below. This is to create emphasis and a change of tempo. I also use *Dúnadh*, the present tense, vivid imagery, repetition, and internal alliteration and rhythm.

### Eriu Addresses the False Kings

*As the False Kings attempt to impost themselves on the people, Eriu moves from Her seat to address the assembled crowd...*

*False speaker, false leader, false man*
*Born of a woman, unworthy of the honour*
*Debased by your rejection of Her womb, Her heart*
*Enemy to half the world*
*Apostate to the other*
*Liar and spreader of lies, like mould and decay*
*Dead among men, unborn among women*
*Unclean among the pure of spirit*
*Firenne rejects you*
*You are false and therefore unable to exist*
*You are the three marks on a king's cheek*
*Your ramparts fall before the anger of the Druids*
*And the Wise Women will make bread from the fire*
*Of your roof,*
*The earth rises against you*
*The stones and bones and blood of the land*

*Reject you and your band*
*Be they born of the land, they are undone*
*Find them shelter in this land, they are undone*
*If they visit this land, they are undone*
*The birds of the air, the food of the earth*
*The spirit of life, the Tuatha and their homes*
*The Tiarna and their laws, the Tír and its being*
*Turn from you, deny you, fast against you*
*The root of your name is poisoned in the ground*
*your stem shall be blighted and the ground salted against you*
*Your tongues fall silent, your limbs weakened, your fruit die untasted on the branch*
*And you are unmourned in the hour of your fall.*
*False speaker, false leader, false man.*
(Geraldine Moorkens Byrne 2016)

While Draíocht Ceoil is a much loved part of Irish Folk Magic, the Rosc represents its ancient origins, and its use for the public well-being. In this era of tumult and war, and sharp political divides, I have many students who are using it as an expression of their activism. It has the great benefit of allowing the expression of political need through magical poetry while also allowing for the expression of our individual emotional response to political wrongdoing. As the basic principle of Irish society was to perform "right action," to be in harmony with Firenne and with the good of the Tuatha and the land, the Rosc enables us to continue that honourable tradition in modern times.

## Chapter 9

# Draíocht Ceoil and Spirituality

Primarily we are concerned with Draíocht Ceoil as a skill, rather than as a spiritual tool. The daily use of Draíocht in recent centuries was unrelated to religion, the majority religion being Catholic. In Ireland, there existed a duality of belief among the population: they remained wholly committed to the mysteries of the Catholic faith while at the same time, believing in the Otherworld, the unseen and supernatural. To claim any aspect of traditional Irish magic traditions as wholly Pagan, or indeed, religious at all, is a false step. While many of the beliefs had their roots in the pre-Christian past, they were part of a very Christian present. However in the last decades as the grip of the church has loosened and people are looking for more individual spirituality, the old gods have become the focus of both scholarship and unique personal Gnosis. Draíocht Ceoil has techniques that have long been used to attune to places, to energy and now to connect spiritually with landscape and culture.

Pagan beliefs found their way in a mitigated form into Early Celtic Church beliefs, but the emergence of the Roman Catholic Church hardened the differences between the two, to a point where to hold dual belief would be inimical to both. Pre-Christian Irish beliefs were polytheistic – Gods were individuals, and complex. They did not ascribe roles to the gods hence there is no "god of war" or "god of love. Each individual god has many attributes. And I would stress, it is not traditional to see the Irish gods as "archetypes," or aspects of a duotheistic or monotheistic deity. Similarly, when people try to conflate Irish Paganism with Christianity, either you demote the Irish gods, or you demote the Christian one – you cannot hold each as equal.

Music has always had some mystical associations; it would be wrong to assert that there is no spiritual connection to music, and deity, in Irish traditions. However, the folk tradition of Draíocht Ceoil has been formed over centuries of actual practice, by people who saw it as a talent and did not associate it with their religion. Draíocht Ceoil should therefore be seen primarily as a skill.

With all that said, there a deep spiritual aspect to Draíocht Ceoil both historically and in modern Pagan practice. In Early Ireland we find poems that represent the claim of kingship and sovereignty over the land itself. In *Homage to Munster* the famed druid and poet, Mogh Ruath invokes the *"Land gentle of passion…land of very beautiful rivers, land of hollows and hills…"* recounting the land's claims to fame, from its *"sword-clashing battles,"* to its *"flowery and mysterious language,"* (a reference to the renown of its poetic class).

In *The Call of Amergin*, we see the claim to not only ownership of land, but to being an incarnation of the land itself. The imagery performs the dual purpose of representing Amergin as indivisible from the land, as well as claiming the strength of the land and nature as his own. From the opening lines of *"I am Wind on Sea, I am Ocean-wave,"* to *"I am a Mountain in a Man,"* the poem is both magical and political. The perfect Irish combination.

Words are repeatedly shown to have the power to transcend this physical reality, to invoke the Otherworld and to act as a conduit between the two. In Imrammic meditation we travel to the Isle of Musicians and the Isle of Poets to access the creativity within our own beings, and to open ourselves to communication with the universe or deity. Even the act of composition itself was seen as entering a liminal space in Old Irish traditions. The *Sanas Cormaic* tells us that darkness and an enclosed space is necessary for the art of composition, separate from writing or performing. This withdrawing in order to compose is both a spiritual and practical act.

## Deity and Music in Old Ireland

There is no specific deity of music in Irish mythology, but music is frequently a tool of several deities, including Dagda, Brigit and Lugh. Irish deities differ from other pantheons in several ways, not least that they (initially, at least) do not occupy a separate, heavenly plane but live on the land itself, are expressions of the sacred landscape, and later, retreat into the land, which becomes itself a gateway to the Otherworld. The Sacred Isles, the mystical places where you might encounter deity, are clearly shown to be connected to this physical reality, through the literature of Voyages (Immrama). The land itself is named for and by deities, from the Paps of Anu to Telltown (named for Tailtiu) and through the *Dinnseanchas* literature, we know of the blurred lines between the land itself and the deities who occupied it.

Dagda, one of the major gods in the Irish pantheon, has a treasured harp, Uaithne, which is not only able to create the three strains of magical music, but also change seasons, avert disaster, and affect behaviour. Its abilities are objectively magical and are employed by Dagda in different ways for the wider good. Made of oak, and luxuriously decorated, it may well be the source of the great respect and veneration accorded to Harpists in Irish society. All its powers from lethal to restorative are demonstrated in *the Cath Tánaiste Maige Tuired* (The Second Battle of Moytura).

In this tale, after a fierce battle the enemy is routed and retreats, but they steal away the harp Uaithne as they do so. The Dagda tracks them, and enters their camp in disguise, calling Uaithne to him. He then plays *Goltraí* music (causing the women to weep and mourn) *Geantraí* (alleviating the sadness of the enemy group) and finally, *Suantraí* (bringing sleep and peace to them).

Dagda uses Uaithne to demonstrate his power and authority, as well as his ability to forgive and show mercy. This story is also significant in that Lugh and Ogma, both famed for their magical skill with music and poetry, choose to accompany Dagda in retrieving Uaithne. The harp itself is revered and treated as an almost sentient being.

The story demonstrates the clear link between music, and the power of deity. It hints at the unifying and reconciling power of music, and as a major figure in the Irish pantheon, the Dagda assumes the role of a unifying force, through music.

Lugh is another deity associated with harping and music, famed for his skill at using music in a magical, supernatural way. In the story *Lugh Comes to Tara,* the hero Lugh uses all his skills to gain entrance to Tara especially his harp skills and in particular a demonstration of all of the three disciplines of music. Music is shown as magical and a way to gain access to liminal, sacred spaces, and is still used like that today. What is also interesting is that the skills performed by Lugh place music on a par with physical and mental prowess. He is a champion of war, but also of building, smithing, poetry and history, as well as a master harpist. Harping is as valued as war skills.

The history of the Ogham script is frequently disputed, with theories falling in and out of scholarly favour. Whatever the actual origins of the script, what is important for our purposes is how it was viewed within the context of early medieval Irish culture. The Irish text *Lebor Ogaim* attributes it to Ogma, a god skilled in poetry and music. The *Lebor Gabála Érenn* and other texts ascribe it to *Fenius Farsa,* the Scythian king. In each case, the purpose of the script is to provide a secret mode of writing, lending itself immediately to magical and spiritual connections. It has had associations with trees since at least the tenth century, and understanding the many coded associations of each of the letters (the Beith-Luis-Nuin) is the basis for magic even today. (Please note, writers such as Robert Graves with his tree calendar are neither Irish, nor based in any real Irish practice). The mythology surrounding Ogma clearly demonstrates the cultural belief that sound is inherently magical, and links sound to music to poetry.

In the Christian era, the development of sacred church music had a profound effect on religion and became a vital part of the expression of belief. Monks chanting in monasteries, the composition of elaborate pieces to glorify the church, the tension between sacred and profane music, all contribute to the power of music to access a spiritual experience.

For modern Irish Pagans, the power of music to express our connection to culture, land, magic and spirituality cannot be overstated.

## Liminal Days and Spaces

"Liminal" is a relatively modern term used to denote a time or place when the barrier between this physical reality and other realities is thin and can be breached. It also means a space that stands at a threshold or boundary, or a transitional space or time through which one passes, from one state of being to another.

Music can be an excellent way of marking and expressing the power of Liminal days or spaces. Obvious examples of these would be Bealtaine, Samhain, Imbolg and Lughnasadh but equinoxes, solstices, eclipses are also generally considered liminal, and if you observe moon stages, which can also be classified as liminal. Places such as Raths, Dúns, tombs, forests, and holy wells are considered to be liminal space. Rites of passage, from childhood to adulthood or from single to partnered status, and so on, can be viewed as liminal. In my Urban Pagan class, I like to point out that communities develop their own liminal days, apart from the established ones.

Draíocht Ceoil can be used both to mark and celebrate this phenomenon and to guide or shape the experience. The former can be seen as devotional or passive – using music and sound to simply announce the event, or to offer praise and thanks.

The latter is active and can be seen as magical or priestly. It uses sound, from voice to instruments, to shape how the person experiences being present in a space or a ritual.

The use of the Prehistoric Horns in early Ireland most likely involved both devotional and priestly activity. They could have been used to set the atmosphere and invoke awe and spiritual awareness in the assembly, as well as simply marking the moment of solstice or burial (we cannot be definitive about the practices and beliefs of the period).

In your modern practice, you can use silence, broken by sound, to create some sense of boundary and threshold; you can compose devotional music and poetry; you can mark astrological and cultural festivals, and you can create community through Draíocht Ceoil. As our ancestors experienced sound in a much quieter world, creating a quiet and peaceful space before punctuating it with music and sound, can go some way to establish a similar experience in modern life. It can mark the period of sound as special, bordered as it were by a period of silence at the beginning and silence at the end.

The type of music or poetry you use as devotional is purely subjective. Don't fall into the trap of recreating Christian style sacred music. You can use any sounds, any expression of joy and belief that you want. It doesn't have to be solemn. It should be the best effort you can offer your deities, but it doesn't have to be perfect. You can make choosing pieces of music an act of devotion in itself, if composing isn't your strong suit. Write a poem, or a prose piece, expressing your belief. Whatever inspiration brings to you is perfectly acceptable.

And performing together is an amazing way to create community and that holds true whether in person or online. A group of people, united in their desire to praise or give respect to their beliefs, singing and playing together on a zoom call may lack the romance of the Hill of Tara at dawn but it is a potent and authentic offering (and also considerably warmer and drier).

Even the effort of listing liminal times, marking them out, being aware of them, trying to mark them with some expression of self, is a valuable spiritual exercise. Expressing belief through sound will open you to a deeper connection with deity.

## Connection with Ancestors

Music is liminal in yet another way. We know it evokes our own memories and connects us to our past. But there is anecdotal evidence that it can act as a gateway to our Ancestors, especially through emotion. This is very evident among the diaspora in particular, with a common story emerging of an intense emotional reaction to a particular song or ballad, heard on a visit to Ireland, catching the person by surprise. Many of the stories share common points – that they were unfamiliar with the song, that they were not in a heightened emotional state, and that they felt something profound, far beyond what the music might reasonably provoke.

And many feel instinctively that it was connected to Ancestral work, even when such veneration was not part of their practice.

Music in my experience can be a powerful part of Ancestral connection, with those whom we knew in life and those who are shadowy figures in our family history. Any music that reminds us of a loved one conjures up their memory and our feelings towards them. Music that is connected to our Ancestors will open us up to more distant connections. If you experience a sudden reaction to music the possibility of Ancestral connections should be considered, and you can actively seek out music from a region or era that might help. The importance of our cultural ties to music cannot be understated.

Poetry and stories are similarly important, and especially in oral form. Listening to a seanchaí (storyteller) can be a very cathartic experience, deeply emotional for people yearning for connection to their heritage. Incorporating live music and stories into Ancestral Veneration adds a new depth to your practice, and supporting indigenous performers is a devotional act.

Music can be used to invite Ancestors into our space. Samhain is an ideal time for this, but it is not limited to that festival. When opening space to Ancestors, music from their region and culture is a respectful greeting.

## Keening

Where Draíocht Ceoil in the folk magic tradition of Ireland meets religion most clearly is in the Keen, or *Caoin*, the lament for the dead. The first keen is attributed to Brigid, who laments the death of her son (Brigid is also associated with a type of whistle, which was used to send messages and was itself magical in nature and purpose). The tradition of Keening for the dead has a long and rich history, from its use as a political, public statement of lament to its status as a part of death in community. You may wish to take a fuller dive into this fascinating topic, but a short overview will be sufficient here.

In its original form, the keen was a public, poetic expression of grief, composed extemporaneously but within an expected structure. This structure was as follows – firstly a genealogy of the deceased, followed by the Eulogy, praise for the deceased and the Lament, expression of Sorrow of those left behind. The keen was generally formed of three motifs: The salutation (introduction), the dirge (verse), and the *gol* (cry).

At one time, keening was an established part of the death rites of any individual. It was performed at the wake, to facilitate the expression of communal grief, and to provide a structure for the same. It is worth bearing in mind that our accounts of the practice for the last four hundred years have been filtered through hostile eyes. British observers called it superstitious and feared what they misinterpreted as unbridled grief. Christian churches considered it too pagan, and an intrusion into their authority over the sacraments of death.

They both missed the underlying psychology and benefits of the tradition.

The music of the keen varied on each occasion that it was sung. However, the pitch in which it was sung was similar (starting low, deep in the throat and rising / falling eventually reaching a high pitch, thus elevating the feelings of the audience). The motifs and diction remained similar from performance to performance, despite the variations in actual melody. Uneven stanzas gave a punchy style, that professional *Mná Caointe* (keening women) utilized to great emotional effect.[46] The *Bean Caoine* (keening woman) could be a family member or a professional keener. In Old Irish society it was usually performed by immediate family members but by the 19th centuries it was a specialized skill, performed by women who had the gift of extemporaneous composition.

The *Bean Caoine* was present at the wake before burial, until the removal of the coffin to the church, and thereafter from the church to the graveside. At the wake, they controlled the expression of grief by both individuals, and the community. Each person arriving at the wake would spend a period of time in mourning at the dead person's side, accompanied by the keening women. When they finished their keen, it was time to move back out into the gathering of the living, and start to pay respects to the family, and then to participate in the funerary games and antics that characterized the Irish wake. The keen also indicated the length of and volume of expression of grief by the community, and provided a shield for the immediate family, keeping their expressions of grief private.

There is a psychopomp aspect to the art of Keening, a sense that the expression of grief and eulogy in the lament aides the passing of the soul during the period of the wake.[47]

There are obvious associations between the *Bean Caoine* and the *Bean Sidhe* or Banshee, the famous foreteller of death among certain Irish families. It is unclear whether the two evolved one from the other, the mortal woman imitating the fairy or whether the mortal tradition is a survival of religious rites of which the *Bean Sidhe* is also part. What is important for our purposes is the use of music to not only control the mechanism of grieving, the use of *Goltraí* to facilitate grief, but music as a conduit from this reality to another.

In modern times, especially for those of us seeking re-connection with authentic Irish spirituality, understanding the nuts and bolts of Draíocht Ceoil, of attuning to sound and opening ourselves to the energy of sound, can be a tool for connection with deity. It is just important to understand that it's not the primary role of the practice, nor is the practice inherently pagan.

The question of ritual can be a vexed one in Irish Witchcraft and Paganism, with many modern practitioners who are exploring Irish indigenous paganism seeking to create new expressions of ceremony and devotional practices. There are no records of ancient ritual, and no way of knowing what our ancestors believed or how they practiced, beyond the clues left to us by archaeology and the early medieval texts. So, all discussion of spiritual rituals needs to take into account that much of it is personal Gnosis, even when based on solid scholarship. We can't say either where magical practice began and spiritual practice ended, when looking at Old Irish society. In modern Irish history, the two coexisted quite happily in the minds of the ordinary person, despite the scorn of the occupying British on one side or the moral strictures of the Catholic Church on the other.

It is not my intention to tell anyone that they cannot conflate religion and witchcraft; only to stress that the two are not synonymous in Irish traditions. My personal practice is to separate the two; I have no need of gods to raise magical energy and frankly I think they would be quite irritated by the intrusion. In matters of public interest, especially when performing a

Rosc, I consider it to be of interest to the gods, and in private matters I think they expect me to deal with it myself. In the case of the former, I might call on them to witness my satire or support it, but in the latter case I would not. Personally, I consider my ancestors to have a greater interest in my personal life and issues rather than gods.

Everyone needs to determine for themselves how they approach this, and how they work. Again, my only rule is that if people declare that their way is the only way, run for the hills.

## Sound and Messages in Meditation

I'm saying "meditation", but we can include any form of communication with deity or any meditation to connect with archetypes and self (Immrama). When we open ourselves to messages, we receive them in many ways. I have received messages through dreams, through Immrama Meditation, through sitting thinking about something else entirely. Many of the exercises in earlier chapters that teach you how to attune to the sound energy of a place or crowd, have the added benefit of making you more responsive in general to messages, and to inspiration (*Imbas*).

Obviously the first stage is to receive a message (*Isteach*), but the next stage is to interpret it, and I tend to put this in the category of *Amach*, of turning an inner sound into an articulated message.

Trying to "hear" messages can feel forced and I would advise against setting out to do so. The most common mistake I see students making is to rush things – after two attempts at journeying, they look for messages and impose interpretations, which are part wishful thinking, part inexperience. There are a few things to bear in mind when tempted to see messages and the first is, we're just not that important. In the scheme of things, the Irish Gods are not overly concerned with your daily life, and they are more interested in hard work than devotion or worship. They demand a lot and give little – your reward is honour, and right action. If you do the work, that is enough. So, no Irish deity is going to throw deep demands and impose commitments on a novice. Remember the *Filí* trained for decades to be considered worthy of any divine inspiration. Patience and a commitment to slow, careful learning are essential tools. It's far more important to develop a depth of commitment to a deity or to magical practice than to be the special chosen one. Special chosen ones rarely turn out to be either special or chosen.

Assuming you've done the work, how do we hear and interpret messages?

The first "message" you hear is when you attune to the energy of a place. It is a song that tells you the energy of that place, about how any entities there might feel about your presence, whether the energy inherently wild or created by humans.

As you become more and more adept, you will receive more complex, and nuanced, messages from places, from crowd or individual energy. You can hear discordant notes, you can hear agitation or sadness, and these general messages are very valuable and inform the kind of working you need to do.

But when we enter into the realm of journeying or trying to connect with entities beyond our norm, then we have to be ready for very complex messages, often ones that use imagery, metaphor and symbolism. That is where we need to be careful to listen, and not rush to project our own interpretations onto it. Messages in dreams are often intensely personal – we talk about Carl Jung's "collective unconsciousness" but in my experience, a meaning that is personal to you trumps any traditional or Jungian interpretation.

For example, my friend dreamt regularly about a bird that would (in her dream) sit on a branch outside her bedroom window and sing noisily every morning. She lived in the inner city, and there was neither a bird nor a branch outside her window, but this was such a vivid dream, it woke her up. She mentioned it to someone who told her it represented messages from beyond, and her connection to the earth. Now this makes sense in general, birdsong often contains messages, but then my friend told all this to her mother who laughed.

Apparently when she was a kid, she used to love a picture that her grandmother had hanging in her house, of a bird singing on a tree branch, while a little girl peeps out the window. Her grandmother had passed three months earlier, and once my friend was reminded of the picture, she realised that to her this was the real meaning. She had the dream precisely once more, when she listened to the actual bird song and felt she had received a message solely for her.

When we hear sounds in dreams, they can mean something quite straightforward – an alarm or siren means a warning and so forth – or they can, as in the example above, be intensely personal or nuanced. The exercises designed to help you be hyper-aware of sound in real life, also help you to notice sounds in dreams or journeys that you might otherwise overlook. These sounds can help you understand the nuances of a message with greater clarity and depth of understanding.

Conversations in dreams are often difficult to recall – this is one thing that can be helped greatly by the exercises for Draíocht Ceoil. You can become better at actually recalling the details, and also at hearing the tone, tempo, or rhythm of speech which helps you to understand the actual message. Just as in real life, the words spoken may be belied by the undercurrents of tone, pitch and tempo. *Isteach* exercises really help with accessing and understanding these nuances. And in general, they help you separate the surface appearances from the underlying truth; concentrate on and listen to the true notes not just the obvious words.

When it comes to encountering deities in dreams or journeying, we also have to be aware that not all is as it appears. When you rely only on visuals and take words at face value, you risk being manipulated. Being aware of sound opens a new dimension of communication within journeys and dreams. The same exercises that ask you to listen beyond the obvious with other people apply to communications with otherworldly entities. Gods may speak to you very plainly – An Morrigan, for example, tends to be fairly clear and straightforward in her messages – but they may also communicate poetically, and through metaphors. An understanding of nuance in language helps here, as does developing your own sense of poetical language.

And entities may pose as deities or take the form that they sense your wishful thinking desires. They may drip honeyed words or frighten you with dire predictions. There are many mischievous entities, and there are entities that like to rebuke anything they perceive as hubris on our part. Listening for the note of truth, for the underlying base note energy in every communication, better prepares you for these encounters. Remember that consent has to be present in any bargain, any commitment, made to deity and you always have the right to withdraw, meditate, consider and make an informed choice. Any entity that presents otherwise is not operating from a place of either Firenne (truth) or honour.

The practice of Draíocht Ceoil can extend beyond the mundane into the spiritual and emotional, and the more we practice in this reality, the better our communication and understanding in the Otherworlds.

## Opening Lines of Communication

When we find ourselves confronted with an entity, whether presenting as itself or as a deity, or archetype, it is a good practice to have a sort of ritualised, standard greeting to hand. The response to such greetings can tell you a lot about what you're dealing with and how to proceed. This practice is based on very old customs, from earliest times, when *Filí* and other notables would greet each other with these standard openings – how the other person responded immediately showcased the depth of their understanding of poetic language.

We do not have to be overly elaborate, but the principle is the same. Memorizing a standard greeting relieves you of the pressure to think of something on the spot, instead you can free up your mind to concentrate on hearing and analyzing what the other is saying. A good greeting should be open to interpretation (you are leaving room for the other to show off some understanding of different layers of meaning). So just saying "Dia Duit" or "Howya," won't do the job. Instead, you should make a statement and ask a question. One example, especially when meeting with an unknown, might be, *"Your arrival has startled me, here in this peaceful place. How come you here, by what means?"*

A reply from one well versed in poetic magic might be, *"My presence alone cannot cause alarm, for I am a rod of peace. How came I here? Not hard to answer – I came by hard work, a long road and my own breath."*

What appears on the surface to be a strange exchange is actually rich in meaning. By calling the place peaceful, you are challenging them obliquely to declare whether they intend disturbing the peace, or not. By asking how they came there, you are asking whether they are a visitor, like you, or if they belong there. If they had replied, I came here through long use, or indeed, I did not approach (or some variant of this) they are telling you they are inherently part of the place, perhaps a spirit of the place. When you examine their reply, they seek to reassure you by calling themselves a rod of peace. However, bear in mind that a rod can have the meaning of spear, or stick, and peace can be imposed through force. They are not saying that they are completely peaceful. They tell you that they came here, ní hansa (not hard to say), through hard work (the long study of a learned person) a long road (over time, or through the long years of study) and "my own breath" can mean "through my own efforts," and also references the magical breath that produces sound, a declaration of proficiency in Draíocht.

You can tailor this basic idea to your own needs. If you are meditating and have set places that you encounter entities (Beach, Forest, Sacred Isles etc). have a standard greeting for each place. You will generally find that you meet certain types in set places, – for example, in Immrama, one encounters Ancestors on a particular sacred isle. To greet an Ancestor, I always used the form of "claiming lineage," e.g. "I am *Gearóidín* (Geraldine) daughter of ..." and list my clans. This prompts the Ancestor to do the same, declaring what branch of the family they are nearest allied to. Even if they are from some link in your tree far back, they will – out of courtesy to the form used in greeting – declare the nearest common descendant known to you.

To greet Deity, or what appears to be deity, I personally use the following, because I believe in combining respect with healthy caution. I would advise this approach with the Sidhe too – although frankly avoiding them altogether is probably the best advice I can give.

*"Honour to you, and respect, and all that is due to you. My eye is brightened and the day is longer, thanks to your presence. What good fortune has brought about this meeting?"*

The single most important piece of this greeting is "and all that is due to you." This acts as a closed phrase, a statement that only what is due to them can be given. This play on words avoids offending them but limits any commitment you might inadvertently make. As mentioned above, this is not an issue with the Gods, who value honour and free consent, but is a potential problem with tricky entities like the Sidhe. By asking what good fortune has brought the meeting, you remain respectful but insist on the right to know why they are interacting with you.

From these examples, I hope you can formulate stock greetings for yourselves that will help you to interact both respectfully and safely.

## Templates for Prayers and Paeans

The use of song and words of praise to honour deity is an age-old practice but nowadays finding a suitable prayer or hymn can be frustrating. There are no "hymns" or prayers per se in Irish Paganism. If our pre-Christian ancestors worshipped in that manner, the record of it is lost to us. What remains to us, however, is a general understanding of the importance of words, the love of Irish poets for complex structures, and the beauty of what prayers remain to us of the early Celtic Christian Church. Rather than claim to reconstruct "authentic" Irish prayers, I think the best approach is to remain as true as we can to the spirit of the enterprise.

A simple construction for a prayer is one that comes to us from the early medieval period and is echoed in Irish prayers ever since. Firstly, the invocation of more than one figure, as in the greeting common in Irish "Dia Duit," (God be with you) and its response "Dia is Muire Duit" (God and Mary be with you). Some devout souls tacked on Patrick, Brigit and random other saints in an excess of holiness. Prayers for Ireland commonly invoked, "Patrick, Brigit and all the saints," while each locality added on its own saint to the list. In Kildare, Patrick took third place in importance to Brigit, the local saint and Conleth, yet another local figure.

Pagans might well look to Brigit, historically our most popular Goddess, as well as Dagda and Danu, and figures such as Lugh, Manannán Mac Lir and of course, An Morrigan. Don't just string them together, choose wisely and make them relevant to you and your practice. Also, *Bandia* (ban -dee-ah) means Goddess, and *Sinsear* (shin-shir) means Ancestor, both useful to invoke if you prefer not to be specific.

Another traditional form used in prayers is "until my dying day," to denote serious commitment and devotion. In many prayers, nature is invoked using metaphors. "God is the tree, and I am the leaf," or some variant of this, was always popular, meaning I belong to this community of devout people or to this particular deity. Prayers were commonly used to bless labour – especially domestic or agricultural labour and to bless the family, near and far.

In modern times we tend to associate prayer with specific ritual times, but our folklore records clearly demonstrate that spiritual blessings were part of everyday social exchanges and belief was intrinsic to the fabric of daily life. On a personal level, I like to give thanks and acknowledgment verbally or through song for moments of beauty and peace; I sometimes feel moved to express a connection to my deities. In those moments, the power of words and poetic form comes to the fore, just as in magical practices.

Here is a favourite type of prayer for me, one which combines the above suggestions and can be used in a variety of ways. I always use some Irish in construction, but you can, of course, adjust to your own level of comfort with that.

*Na Déithe a beith liom* (The Gods are with me)
*Dagda is Danu, is Bríd Alainn* (Dagda and Danu, Beautiful *Bríd*)
I am the leaf on the branch of
their strong rooted tree.
I offer thanks for the joy in birdsong
and the whispers of the wind.
*Siúl liom, Siúl liom, Siúl liom* (walk with me)
Walk with me.

This simple structure can be adapted to be a prayer of entreaty, or of praise and so on.

## Ancestral Prayers

In Irish Polytheism, the traditional view of the Gods is that they are largely unconcerned with human needs, and instead are interested in what we can offer – right action, in particular. For many coming from a Christian or other mainstream religious viewpoint this can be hard to adjust to, because supplication and prostration form the basis of the relationship with deity in those religions. I don't beg my Gods, and I would only ask for help to do things that are of public importance, and only when I've done my share of the work. I will acknowledge their presence and express gratitude for that, but when it comes to my personal life, I turn to those who have a vested interest – my Ancestors.

A prayer to the Ancestors is a little more personal and should open with a greeting. Remember many of your more immediate ancestors will not be Pagan, for quite a long line back. I tend towards a respectful, Dia Duit, or Do Dhéithe Duit (God be with you, or Your gods be with you). I ask them to be with me, to listen to me, to take an interest in my problems, for the sake of our common names (shared ancestry) and then I would end by thank them for their continued support.

*Do Dhéithe Duit, mo shinsir (Your gods with you, my ancestors)*
*fada is fadó, bíonn sibh in mo chroí (Long and long ago, ye are (always)in my heart)*
*I honour ye, I give thanks for ye*
*I lay my problems before ye*
*I pray for your intersession*
*Grant me your wisdom and*
*aid me in right action*
*for the sake of our common names.*

# Chapter 10

# Practical Exercises

## Raising Your Voice

There is one barrier to Draíocht Ceoil that many do not expect until the time comes to practice and that is self-consciousness. When we were children, we raised our voices and sang, screamed, cried, laughed at full volume. Almost immediately, we were told to be quiet.

As a mother of two, I am guilty of this. No one wants to rear kids who are loud and rude and intrude on the peace of others. But in our haste to put limits on the noise, we must not forget to provide space where they can let loose and shout. Here we are, adults, afraid to look foolish or be judged because we are too loud, talk too much, let enthusiasm show in our conversations. Perhaps we don't stand up for ourselves or others, perhaps we swallow down insults and hurts. Maybe it's just that we deny ourselves the joy and pleasure of making noise. But whatever form it takes, it can make us too timid to plunge headfirst into the magic of sound.

It's easier to be passive, to bathe in a sound bath or listen to music, to practice *Isteach* at the expense of *Amach*, and it's a pity. Valuable as listening is, it is only half the story. Without *Amach* we cannot be effective, and it will only be as powerful as our confidence allows.

I cannot stress this enough – you do not have to have talent for music, only an appreciation of the power of sound. Make music, and don't worry about whether it is in tune or out of tune. Roll words off your tongue, savour their bitterness and feast on their sweetness. Pluck the strings of a guitar and hit the bells. Be the person singing along to the radio at traffic lights. Explore every sound, man-made or in nature and then try to make your own version of it. Be loud. Even if you have to go somewhere to be alone, to be brave enough, it counts. Tell yourself that you are allowed to be noisy, you deserve to be heard and repeat it as often as you need to.

You cannot be a virtuoso on any instrument without practice and the same is true of Draíocht Ceoil. The exercises in this book are not one-offs – they are intended for you to use again and again, to adapt and make part of daily routine, so that your mindset changes. Eventually, some things become second nature, and you will no longer have to consciously work at it but that takes time. The most adept practitioner started where you are starting, and don't let anyone pretend differently. Having an innate talent or affinity for this practice is all very well, but it will be half-baked and ineffectual without rigorous, daily practice. This is something our *Filí* predecessors knew.

If you're thinking, "Ach, I'll get to those boring exercises later" ...start now. Go on. Practice being in crowds and feeling the energy. Wallow in magical energy in both *Brí* and *Bua,* practice *Isteach* and *Amach,* and do the exercises as you move forward. Even if you think you "do it instinctively," or that you've touched on these things in your current practice, don't skip the steps. There is a difference in conscious, intentional action. You are actively choosing Draíocht Ceoil. The practice of Draíocht Ceoil is something that should permeate every area of your daily life – less a technique to occasionally employ and more an intrinsic way of being, of living in harmony (pun intended) with the world around you.

My advice is to resist the temptation to graft Draíocht Ceoil on to eclectic paths. You can, of course, incorporate your spirituality into your individual practice, but first establish a foundation in the tradition. Respect the core of it, the role it played in Irish life and society for generations. In the next chapters, I will describe techniques for cleansing, making tools, examples of workings and explore the use of Draíocht Ceoil in hexing and healing.

### *Exercises*

The following are designed to make you aware of sound, and its effect on you and to practice the basics needed for Draíocht Ceoil.

### *Isolating Sound in Everyday Situations*

Wherever you find yourself, there will be background noise. In the supermarket or shopping centre or Gym you will have music playing, announcements over tannoys, dominant sounds that we associate with those places. A busy street will sound of traffic – car engines, buses, horns. In Nature, you will have birdsong or a river, again some dominant sound that becomes the main "song" of that place.

But beneath that obvious noise will be layers of other sounds, like an orchestral piece where one section carries the melody, but each section of instruments adds their counterpoint and harmonies. Our first task is to listen to these other, more subtle sounds and follow them. Isolate and identify the sound, then listen to it and how it contributes to the whole (if you have every followed an orchestral score, it's the same principle). This refines your listening skills and can be done anywhere. Make a note of what sound you followed, what was its pitch, tempo and how it made you feel.

If you're walking around, an interesting riff on this exercise is to physically follow the sound, try to wander where it leads you. I have had many interesting and intriguing experiences doing this – from seeing things I might otherwise have missed to meeting people and finding places.

### *Music and Emotion Exercise*

Listen to as many types of music as you can and especially music that you normally would not choose. Move away from the "same old, same old," and try to surprise your brain. The genre of music doesn't matter, nor does the length of the piece.

Note down the effect each has on you – what makes you sad, upbeat, uneasy, irritated and so on. Note your reaction to different instruments, to different rhythms and to the various parts of each piece. Note how changes from one part to another affects you (e.g. from the verse to chorus, or from a section of a classical piece to another).

Ask yourself, is this what the composer intended? Are you having a reaction that others would share, or is this an unusual reaction? Reacting the same way as others proves the connectivity of human experience, and reacting differently proves the uniqueness of each individual. Both are good things.

Build up a repertoire of tunes and pieces that you associate with different emotions; these can form a valuable shorthand for you to use later. When you construct a spell, your ability to draw on certain musical forms is similar to the ability of the *Filí* to draw on poetic forms. These are the structures that enable us to build, while leaving space for inspiration.

### *Conscious Listening and Information*

Note: This may be difficult for people with certain processing or neurodivergent issues, and that's okay. Do not beat yourself up trying to perfect something that is simply too difficult or uncomfortable. However, within your own abilities, I would suggest trying the following and seeing how you get on. There's no medal for making yourself miserable, these exercises are suggestions not requirements. But if you find it of any benefit having tried it, you can make a decision from there.

Listening to information-dense broadcasts, podcast, audio books or news articles is the ideal way to practice conscious listening. Conscious listening engages us in two ways, the intake of information and the processing of the same. It's an important workout for the brain. Information that interests us obviously engages the brain, so vary the content. You want to practice listening but also, processing the information and testing your retention of the same.

The Irish *Filí* were trained to remember oral history, stories, poetry and law. This training is largely beyond us in the modern world (frankly, I have trouble remembering my pin for my credit card, let alone large tracts of text or data). But we can still flex that brain muscle and it's an important exercise for Draíocht Ceoil.

Your first task is to remain focused on the information, not letting your attention stray. If you realize you've missed or half-listened, rewind and try again. Train yourself to attach importance to that act of focusing.

The next task is to process the information. Be aware of its effect on you, your reaction to it, what thoughts it provokes as you listen (try to quickly note these thoughts and ideas and set them aside for further pursuit).

The final one is to test your retention of the data – what overall message or news did you receive, what details can you remember, what struck you as important and relevant and what was mere filling, opinion pieces, padding, speculation and so on.

The more you practice this kind of listening, the better able you are to evaluate a situation quickly and accurately, and the better you'll be at critical analysis. The other benefit is to strengthen your understanding of the manipulation of emotion or opinion through words. The next exercise can be combined with this task.

### *What People Say versus What People Mean*

This is another critical thinking listening exercise, and one that benefits everyone, including neurodivergent students – in fact, they often bring a unique and discerning ear to this.

Listening to what people say is a surprisingly uncommon thing. We tend to apply a shorthand to people that we know – they say things and part of our brain interprets what they say according to the role they play in our lives, or the way we feel about them. This extends to people we think we know like politicians, celebrities and so on. When someone we dislike speaks, even if they say something reasonable it irritates us. If someone we like makes a remark that should annoy us, we tend to gloss over it and repackage it to be inoffensive. Developing a critical ear is important for magic in general, and vital for Draíocht Ceoil. It also ties into the idea of understanding a situation completely, from beginning to end, before meddling in it magically.

Listen carefully to what people say, and note whether their tone, flow of words, rhythm, and tempo match what their words are designed to convey. Listen to what they don't say, – for example, if asked to recommend a mutual acquaintance for something, they may say "Oh, they're very nice" but not "they're very honest and reliable." If they are telling you gossip, pay attention to what they emphasize and what they downplay. It may be conscious or unconscious, but we tend to present and receive information in a way that serves our purpose or confirms our bias.

There are many verbal and non-lexical clues to the meaning and emotions behind what is being said including repetition of words, stumbling over words, avoiding words, using fillers like um and ah, and changes in tempo and volume. Listening beyond words opens up these layers to us.

### *Meditation on Specific Sounds*

Taking one sound or word and meditating on it, its effect on you and the meaning you attach to it, is another exercise that you can benefit from at any stage in your journey. Because of my – to the meaning and emotions behind what is being said. Because of Misophonia, I've always had a tendency to fixate on a word until its sound loses all meaning and I'm not entirely sure it's a word at all anymore. But this tendency has made me extremely aware of words.

The easiest way to start is to pick a sound you hear all the time and that you can reproduce. As an example, a pen that you click to access the nib – close your eyes and click, click, click. Leave a space between each click, then do it in rapid succession. Listen to what your brain is telling you, what images or thoughts or memories it throws up. Don't resist, just follow the train of thought.

For words, for preference pick a word that is in everyday use. A word like "teacher," "boss," "family," can harbour rich and complex associations, both pleasant and difficult. Lean into whatever your brain throws up, repeating the word in varied ways, accents, speeds, volume, rhythms and allow your mind to centre on it. Follow it wherever it takes you, and in both non-verbal and verbal sounds, try to dissect why you react to it – is it the meaning you have attached to it or the inherent sound itself? Concentrating like this on one sound helps us experience flow state. Flow state increases our receptiveness to meditation and journeying, as well as ability to focus our will on a desired outcome.

These exercises can be done separately, in rotation, regularly or sporadically as suits but to begin with at least, I would strongly suggest doing them regularly, and one at a time until you feel comfortable doing them. Practice them as you explore Draíocht Ceoil until you build up an innate understanding of the techniques involved.

# Chapter 11

# Cleansing Space

With all the exercises and outlines for magical workings, we start with intentionality. Create a clear aim for the working, spend time thinking through the repercussions and pitfalls, proceed once you are satisfied you have a solid understanding of the situation.

## Cleansing Technique

One of the most practical ways to use Draíocht Ceoil is to clear space before attempting to tune into sound, or to make a space safe and to restore a balanced energy after practice sessions. The following is the most traditional way to cleanse the energy of your space.

This same technique is used to dedicate a space, to cleanse a house of negative accumulated energy and so on. What differs from one application to the next is what base note you wish to end on. You want a note that will bring a clean, neutral energy. In a place of business that will be a higher, more charged note than in a bedroom while a living room will differ from a space needed for creative pursuits. These differences can be subtle but if you find a note trying to assert itself, don't fight it – let the space tell you what it needs.

Bear in mind High (charged energy), Medium (calm and balanced) and Low(soothing) and be careful not to introduce one at the expense of another more suitable note.

## Driving Out Negative or Staid Energy

At its most basic, anything that creates noise will work. You can bang pots and pans, if that's all you have to hand.

To cleanse an entire building, you need to work from the top down, from one side of the house to another (back to front, or vice versa). You should have a front or back door open, driving out negative energy in front of you, and out into the air.

To cleanse a smaller space, you open a door or window, and drive the energy from the furthest point, out in front of you, and out into the air. If you are occupying space in a shared building and are only working on the energy of your personal space, do not drive the energy out into the shared areas of the place. Drive it out into the air, to disperse, either through a window or a door, even if you have to work down a corridor or hall to do so. Be mindful of the rights of others.

If you just make noise and push unwanted energy out, you will succeed in making the energy of that space cleaner, less stagnant. But with a bit of preparation, you can do so much more than that. If you think ahead and plan out what exactly you want to achieve, you can do a lot more than merely "clean."

Think about the primary purpose of the space. A bedroom should be a calm place to rest, but perhaps you also want it to be a place for sex and desire. If you wish to have a relaxing, pleasant energy in a shared space, you have to consider the feelings of the others using it. If you want the space to be somewhere to create, or an energetic place of business, that requires a different approach.

There is often a liminal moment in cleansing as well, a gap between merely clean energy and energy that is positively charged with intent. This presents an interesting opportunity to evaluate your needs and how to organize this energy.

### Shared versus Personal Space

The first issue to consider is who has primary rights to a space. Are you a guest in a space? Is it yours but you have paying tenants? While we all have a right to feel comfortable in our space, we need to consider the rights of those around us. Some spaces are obviously private – your bedroom, if you are the sole occupant, is indisputably yours in terms of energy – but shared spaces have to be open to all. Just as when we talked about approaching a space to attune to its natural energy, we are not entitled to enter other people's spaces.

## What Are You Hoping to Achieve?

Most of us experience shared living space at some point, where competing needs must be balanced. Hard enough at the best of time, but if they are not people whose company you enjoy, then this becomes harder again. So how to move through this situation with respect for everyone's needs?

There are two approaches, and it just depends on which suits your circumstances. When I rented (and I have shared houses with a wide variety of great, good and absolute nightmare humans) if I had a good relationship with my cohabitors, I imbued my spot on the couch or my place at the table with positive sound energy. If it was a more uncomfortable situation, then I created a protective bubble around myself and used a particular song to reinforce this in moments of tension.

I also made sure to air out the energy of the whole house regularly. For a lot of my working life, I had Monday off and that became the day when I would usually take half an hour to drive out accumulated *Bua* from us all living together. It didn't completely prevent fights or discontent, but it did enable me to coexist with people and not feel overwhelmed or undermined by their energy.

Nuance is important. Continuing with our earlier example of the bedroom, its most obvious use is for sleep, which corresponds to the *Suantraí* strain of magic. But by adding in a strain of *Geantraí* – sweetness and happiness – you leave space for love, physical desire and sex as well as other forms of intimacy. A room charged only for sexual intimacy is not conducive to sleep, rest and withdrawal. Similarly, a room charged only for slumber stifles and dampens sexual and physical intimacy. Both energies require a space.

Starting with cleansed or neutral energy, you will now begin to construct a layer of intent, using sound and words. The first step is to find words that clearly state your desired outcome. This is harder than you might imagine, especially when you need to use the space in more than one way.

You may compose your own melodies but if you're not particularly inclined to do so, choose music that already conveys what you're trying to achieve. And if it is music that has a particular emotional resonance for you, so much the better. Many pop songs have a blend of different strains, as does classical music. Modern music has an advantage in that it tends to compress complex emotions and desires into a short, fully formed piece (much like poetry). But the right music can be any piece that works for you.

Or you can opt to use individual sounds, blending high notes and medium/low, chanting words of power at those pitches. My recommendation is to experiment regularly and see what is the most effective for you. Practicing different approaches will stand you in good stead when trying other aspects of Draíocht Ceoil.

### Example: Cleansing a Living Room (Shared Space)

My technique is to write out in full what my end result should be.

I want the living room to be calm, a room I feel comfortable to enter, welcoming, relaxing. I want to feel like I can leave my stuff there without worrying about it being disturbed. I want it to be a place where we can have a laugh and chat.

The relaxing element mentioned above is *Suantraí* and the social aspect would be *Geantraí* – I need to find music that suits both. Which is more important to me? In my twenties, without a doubt it would be *Geantraí*, merry making and socializing. In my fifties, *Suantraí* is more important to me, but I still want a welcoming sociable element there. Which strain is dominant depends on which you want to prioritize.

I need to condense what I want to achieve into carefully selected words, to convey as much as possible as simply and clearly as possible.

You can choose individual words like, "Comfort, Peace, Welcome," and perhaps translate this into Irish *"Sólás, Síocháin, Fáilte,"* (roughly pronounced So-loss, Shee-uh-coyne, Fall-chuh). You can chant this, sing it, set it to music. You can add an extemporaneous element by chanting and letting your unconscious mind set it to music. This is something similar to the folk tradition of chanting while churning or spinning. You can take a melody you feel is ideally suited and set those words to it. Try it all.

Another technique is to compose a poem, using those words as a base and sing or chant that in the same way. This adds complexity to the working. If like me you are a poet by nature, it's the more natural approach. But one way is not better than another, both are rooted in both older Irish practices and folk magic traditions, and trying various techniques until you hit on your preferred approach is highly recommended.

The poem (in English but with some Irish words) might look like this.

Here, in the place I dwell
*Sólás* is my companion and my strength
My strength brings *Síocháin*, for me
and for all who share the shelter of this roof -
under which you will find hospitality,
a *Fáilte* before you,
Here in the place I dwell

Note how it is A) written in the present tense B) uses definite statements (e.g. ...you will find hospitality rather than "I want" or "I hope.") The first and last line "close" or complete the verse (*Dúnadh*). These old poetic forms have inherent power, adding emphasis and immediacy to the words.

You can beat out a rhythm as you play, using whatever is to hand. You can add stresses to different words, increasing their importance and use tempo and pitch to invoke the relevant strains, in this case *Geantraí* or *Suantraí*. You can sing it three times, for example. The first emphasizing the most important of your strains (in this example, *Suantraí*) the second emphasizing the secondary one, *Geantraí* and the third time returning to *Suantraí* to establish its dominance.

Now you are using words, music, stress/rhythm and performance all combined to amplify your intent.

## Instruments

Your access to musical instruments is another factor to consider. If you can play an instrument, you may want to play all or part of your song yourself and add yet another personal layer to the sound spell you create. Or you may associate certain instruments with a particular action. I have a green kazoo that has made many an appearance in classes, and which I find ideal for hexing. A hexing drum is also a valuable tool. I have Tibetan cymbals which produce the ideal "medium-low" note for introducing a calming, peaceful energy. I can play several instruments, most of them quite badly, and using them definitely adds a deeper connection to any working.

If you don't play any instruments there are quite a few options that don't require technical skill. You can buy musical "wooden spoons" that are very easy to play, as are cymbals or bells, where you want to produce notes rather than play melodies. While playing a Kalimba (thumb piano) properly does require skill, they are capable of producing beautiful tones that can add greatly to your sound. While we can use instrument from other cultures for their tonal qualities, do not ascribe magical or spiritual properties to them that may be at odds with their cultural use.

### *Practical Exercise 1 – Changing the space you are in right now*

Ideally you should have a physical space that you are familiar with and have the right to occupy. First, ensure its energy is as neutral as possible. Cleanse using sound as outlined earlier.

If you don't have access to a comfortable space or would like to try this later, be ready with a psychic space – create a "room" around you and use sounds as outlined in the exercise but in your own head. Work through these steps:

- Attune to the sound of the space.
- Decide where you want to take that energy – charge it, soothe it etc.
- Choose the noise best suited to achieving that effect.
- Make that noise!!

In the example below, we are going to charge the energy then bring it down to a soothing, calm stage, working our way through High, Medium, and Low notes, changing tempo as we go and finally added spoken sound.

Start with High Notes, these should bring a more energized, lighter feel. This can be achieved with instruments such as tin whistles or voice. Speed up rhythm and tempo, adding stresses on the first and last beats of the phrase (this makes the energy more charged). Add non-lexical spoken sound (e.g. lilting "*hey-deidle, didle-dum, i-dl-ee dee, dum-die-dle*")

Now bring the tone down to Medium Notes. This is a calmer energy, but still upbeat. The sound of violins, the voice, or a higher pitched *Bodhrán* (14") all work well.

Maintain the rhythm and tempo. Add non-lexical spoken sound (Humming, nonsense words, lilting) and finally switch to Low Notes, taking the energy down to a contemplative, solemn place. Instruments like cello, clarinet, low pitched *bodhráns* are ideal as is the lower register of the piano. Slow down the tempo, only emphasize beats that are five or six apart. Add non-lexical spoken sound or chant a word e.g. Síocháin (peace).

I have done variations on this exercise with students, working individually and end masse, with great success. Students have also found it a good exercise to do out and about, often putting in headphones to filter out the ambient sounds around them and concentrating on visualizing the space, and performing the exercise, internally. And yet another variation to try is taking each section one at a time and practicing transitioning from high to low, low to medium and so on.

In between these practice sessions, be sure to clean your space and restore a neutral energy.

### *Practical Exercise 2 – Creating a sound spell for a specific place*

Pick one place, and prepare it by removing any accumulated, stagnant or negative energy.

Decide on a desired outcome. Pick something fairly straightforward to begin, one clear objective. Spend time on this objective, visualizing it and outlining to yourself why you want or need it, what benefits you expect from it, what problem it solves.

Pick one word that expresses the objective and identify which strain of music best aligns with it. From that, choose whether you need high, medium or low pitch (bearing in mind the rough delineation of High being vibrant and charged, Medium being calmer and comforting, and Lower ranging from healing and calming, to disturbing).

For this we are attempting a simple sound spell. One word, one main objective, one pitch and one of the traditional magical strains of music.

A very good example would be to place a protection (ward) on a window or door. This naturally limits both the size of the space involved and narrows down the objective to "protection" and you can try words like "safety," "closed," or "fortress." You can try to pick a word that has multiple layers of meaning, or that has layered associations. Perhaps these associations are only apparent to you, but they will add depth to it. You are not expected to understand the etymology and semantics involved, but more to capture the spirit of the poetic language.

One word I personally find powerful is the Irish word *Dún,* which can mean to close as in dún an doras (shut the door) or can mean a fort (as in place names such as Dún Laoghaire, the Fort of Laoghaire. The dual connotations of that sound *"Dún"* (pro. Doone) provide me with a sense of closure, safety, protection, enclosure, and stronghold. The long vowel sound lends itself to slow chanting, but the word is short enough to work for quick urgent stresses as well.

Once you have chosen your word, decide on your "song" – a chant, a melody, with or without percussive accompaniment. For this exercise keep it simple and decide on how long you want it to be. Three to five minutes is a good target, but you can adjust according to your personal needs. I have times when I can concentrate for hours and at other times, five minutes would be an eternity. Intensity and clarity of intention outweigh the time spent performing.

***Practical Exercise 3 – Creating a complex sound spell***

Now it is time to create your own multi-layered sound spell. To recap the steps above – you need to cleanse the energy and start with a neutral base, then set out clear objectives and take the time to work through the ramifications of any outcome you wish to attempt.

Assuming you have now a clear plan, you need to prioritize these objectives. When there are several elements to be balanced, one is often the priority. Occasionally all of them will be equally important. You need to consider this carefully.

When you have identified the importance, you wish to place on each desired outcome, then match it to a strain of *Suantraí, Geantraí* or *Goltraí*. If the connection is not obvious, just do your best. Trial and error are necessary while you build up experience.

To take a new example, let us look at a workspace within the home. This is introducing a different energy and purpose, which can affect the overall *Bua* of the house. You don't want your workspace to be too domestic and you definitely don't want the rest of your home to feel like an office. You need to contain the energy of the working area and charge it differently from the rest of your house. You need to set a clear boundary, and you need a certain amount of bustling, highly charged energy in that space – a sleepy relaxed energy might be nice in your living room, but no one wants to go face down into the keyboard mid-afternoon.

Equally, you don't want the space to feel frenetic. The highly charged energy of *Geantraí* needs to be tempered with *Suantraí* but in this case, *Geantraí* is the more dominant one.

What type of work you need to do would be a factor too. This holds true for any working space – playrooms, craft rooms, kitchens etc. If you are mainly in administration, there is a different level of interaction with the public than someone who is on zoom calls with colleagues or customer. All these things affect how you use the space and what kind of energy you need there.

Another consideration is whether or not you'll be using the space for sound. If you'll be constantly talking, or recording within that space, do bear this in mind.

Let us pretend, for the sake of demonstration, that you have a space that needs to be very energized, sales oriented (*Geantraí*) on the one hand, but also needs to leave space for creativity (marketing, social media, design) which requires a dollop of *Suantraí*. If you are engaged in work that includes counseling or dealing with people in a moment of stress or grief, *Goltraí* is important. Sorrow, the acknowledgment of grief, and even outright lamenting, all have their place.

Now you have considered all these aspects, the next step is construction. For me, it is natural to use Irish poetic forms. I am an Irish poet, and this part of my heritage has always fascinated me. But while it is a good way to root yourself in the tradition, it is not necessary to strictly follow the conventions of poetry.

An exception to this is if you are composing a Rosc – a Rosc needs to conform to specific rules. And you cannot throw words on a page and claim they follow one of the Irish poetic forms. But you can create your own verse, in your own style, and express your intent in whatever form feels most appropriate.

While you may rely solely on the spoken word, for this exercise we are going to layer music, words and stress (rhythm) to create the whole. You might also consider adding nonsense words, or lilting, as you practice this exercise.

Choose your melody. It should have passages that correspond to the strains you wish to invoke. The dominant strain should also be the dominant mood of the music.

Compose your verse, containing words that you feel convey the desired outcome, put together into a whole that shows clearly what you want for that space. Perform the sound spell, repeating it with additional stresses on the important points. You can use the techniques of lilting highlight the mood of the music.

Your final repetition should be very strong, clear and "targeted" – you should close the space, just as the technique of *Dúnadh* in poetry was considered to "close" a verse. The energy you are raising is to remain in that space, self-contained. Constructing your verse with the *Dúnadh* (first and last phrase the same) and performing the verse with the same emphasis and delivery the first and last time are two techniques that are effective, especially combined.

The applications of Draíocht Ceoil are myriad but this basic practice of cleansing, and then charging the energy of your space with intent, is the best starting point for all other uses. In the next chapter, we will look at some outlines for various workings including creating tools and creating wards.

## Chapter 12

# Outlines and Examples

The following are practical outlines for using Draíocht Ceoil in different ways. This is not an exhaustive list but a starting point for you to begin to build your practice. In previous chapters we looked at tuning into the magical energy of a place, raising energy, changing energy, dealing with crowd energy and the concepts of *Isteach* and *Amach*. We've looked at how to use volume (whisper, song, roar) as well as tempo, rhythm and stresses to layer energy and we have explored using words in spell construction.

Now let's take a look at some specific techniques for practical workings. You should utilize all the tools already looked at, to add depth and strength to any working.

### Imbuing an Object with Magical Intent by Using Draíocht Ceoil

There are many reasons to use objects in magical workings, from hexes and wards around your living space, to creating tools. A tool might include an object imbued with intent that you centre your spell around e.g. a candle that will be burned as part of your working. This technique is also used to create a talisman or ward, whether to leave permanently in your space or carry around with you.

One of the best and most traditional ways to do this is through Draíocht Ceoil. You can use sound alone or you can use words of power, or a combination of both. I personally think of it as bathing the object in sound energy, when using non vocal sound and I envisage the use of words as amplifying the effect, as well as refining it. By refining it, I mean making it more targeted, more specific.

If I was to do a healing spell using a candle imbued with the intent, the music/non vocal sound would create the background atmosphere e.g. of healing, repair, or renewal. But to make it specific to an individual, the most effective way is to add words.

If, however, I was to create a ward to protect a room, the use of music/non lexicon sound alone would be sufficient, although I may choose to add words as an extra layer.

This is purely my personal approach; you can do whatever suits your own way of working. Practicing will help you to find a comfortable way of working before you create more complex spells.

One question I get asked quite a lot is, how do you know when the job is done? Ah, if only there was a light that would turn green to tell us the object is now fully charged and ready for use! You have to trust yourself and the process. Set a time limit on your work, and make sure you build up to that moment. Hitting a crescendo, both in volume and tempo, and tying it to your *Dúnadh* will give you a natural moment of closure. If you feel unsure, or dissatisfied, wait for a while before using the object. When you do, trust your instincts – it will either feel ready to use or it won't. If you think you may have missed the mark, just cleanse the item and start again. Practice makes perfect and there is no shame in trying again.

## Creating a Personal Ward by Using Sound Only

A ward is a protective item that will set a boundary around a person, place or item: it can be permanent, portable, large or small. They are an integral part of folk magic and one of the best ways to create one is using sound. Sound can permeate the very bones of a ward, making it a potent protective spell. For beginners, it can be an excellent starting point to try out different layers of sound, and different ways of creating sound.

Any item can become a ward. If it's something you want to carry with you, obviously choose something small but that's about the only restriction. I would add, if it's to be permanently placed in a room or space, don't choose candles that might be lit and burned, wasting all your hard work! (I may or may not have found this out the hard way.)

Once you have chosen your item, the next step is to choose the sound. The aim is protection, and to create a secure environment (please take note of the points raised in the section on shared space in Chapter 2).

Ideally you want a rich sound, thinking in terms of bathing the item in sound, soaking it in reverberations and tones, and enriching it with sound. Avoid overly upbeat or melancholy melodies, or any discordant sounds. Aim for soothing, warm, rich tones and sound. You can pick a piece of music that you love or choose instruments that will create the effect you desire – both are perfectly valid approaches.

Voice alone is rarely as effective as using instruments, unless you're blessed with a particularly rich timbre vocally. Sounds that work well include Tibetan cymbals, low pitched drum tones, cello music, choral music, orchestral music, gongs and hang drums. Pay attention to tempo and volume. You want calm, not frenzied or erratic and peace, so avoid reaching too loud a crescendo.

In my experience, the most effective approach is to expose the item to magical sound energy for at least ten to fifteen minutes. When I have time to put a lot of effort and planning into wards, I pick several pieces that I feel suit the working, and leave the item in a room with that music playing, for hours before I start the business of directly imbuing it with specific energy. Think of it as marinating the item, letting it soak in a suitable sound environment.

Then I will direct sound at it in a more concentrated form, using something like the Tibetan bells, or *Bodhrán*. This is when I will be intentional and deliberate, willing it to "hold" the sound, and retain it, for a specific purpose (in this example, protection).

As with all descriptions of personal workings in this book, this is my way of doing it. There is nothing wrong in finding a way that suits you, or that you feel confident performing.

### Adding Words

I find that a general protection ward done with sound alone is very effective, if the situation requires more nuance – e.g. when you are operating in a shared space – words are the best way to ensure your ward does exactly what you want, and no more. Rather than composing a long or complex spell, wards tend to be more effective when you use short, punchy sentences, poems or even simply using a carefully chosen word or words. If you tend towards epic poetry, go for it – but experiment with short, firm statements as well.

I once made a portable charm for a person who needed help in social situations. They found navigating friendships and group dynamics difficult. The "fault" lay on both sides: they were by their own admission, very sensitive and their friends were inclined to overlook or forget their difficulties and become impatient with them.

After talking through the issue, it became clear that they had a very fixed idea of what friendship should be and remarked that they wished they could be less reactionary and their friends more sensitive. Using this as the starting point, I reduced the entire issue to *Cairdeas*, the Irish word for friendship. I created a ward out of a key ring, a gift connected to the friend group that they were having most trouble with. The music I chose was a song they all loved, and I placed the key-ring on top of the speakers of the CD player (yes, I'm old) and played the song along with a selection of hits from the same era, the time when this group first met and socialized together.

I then choose to use my *Bodhrán*, placing the item directly inside the rim while using a leather tipped beater to sound out the deepest, most resonant note of the drum, then manipulating the skin through a series of notes rising to a slightly higher pitch. I repeated this progression three times and then intoned the word "*Cairdeas*" three times while hitting the deepest note again. The progression of tones from lowest to a higher pitch was to raise the energy surrounding the issue of friendship, to uplift and lighten it, while still remaining in a very resonant, rich tonal landscape. The sound of the drum and word together "sealed" the spell into the item.

I then returned the key ring to the CD player and let it sit there through another cycle of music. My friend carried it with them and found a resolution to their issues with that group, and a renewal of ties with other people from the past, which gave them more confidence and a wider circle to rely on. At this time, they still carry that key ring with them (and gave permission for the description above).

## Draíocht Ceoil for On-the-Spot Protection

There are several useful techniques for using sound energy as protection when out and about, from creating a talisman imbued with energy (see above) to using a piece of music as a talisman in itself.

For the former, use a melody that makes you feel safe. My take on this is to have one song that I use when feeling overwhelmed, one I use if I feel nervous and yet another if I feel physically unsafe. There's an element of placebo effect in this – the moment I begin to use them, I feel better. But the magical aspect comes from hours of work, listening to the song (*Isteach*) and imbuing it with protective energy. When needed I use *Amach* – I hum them or sing them (sometimes out loud and sometimes in my own head, depending on how odd it would appear to burst into song).

Traditionally whistling or humming in folk stories was both protection from, and a way of summoning, the Sí and other otherworldly creatures while songs such as lullabies provided protection. So be careful using this technique on dark country roads at night, or when passing by raths and duns. I am not joking. In those circumstances, make sure that your chosen melody is wholly protective, and be intentional in using it.

## Draíocht Ceoil, Divination and Meditation

The right soundtrack can help with many things from meditation to spell casting, and divination especially benefits from the use of sound. If using a divination technique that involves a meditative state and opening oneself to *Imbas*, such as fire gazing, music that opens you to inspiration is ideal. It makes the mind receptive to messages, in much the same way as it helps with Immrama meditation. But the right piece may not necessarily be an obvious choice. It doesn't have to be a quiet, slow piece at all. In fact, sometimes a piece that challenges your mind can overcome blockages in both divination and meditation.

One such piece is Donnacha Dennehy's *Grá agus Bás*[48] (Love and Death) which is filled with challenging, unexpected progressions against a rich, emotive vocalization. It is a piece to lean into, to let your imagination run free with. It makes the "world music" of new age popularity pale by comparison. Embrace the difficult, especially in divination and active journeying.

Experiment with different musical forms. I found that when the music is difficult to ignore it seems to free up an unconscious part of my brain. I have also experimented with drumming tracks, high frequency bells and other instruments – don't be afraid to explore lots of different types and genres of music and sound.

Also, as your practice of Draíocht Ceoil deepens you may find that messages come to you in the form of songs, snippets of lyrics, or intriguingly repetitive and insistent notes. You can understand the "code" of these notes by applying your knowledge of sound.

First pay attention to pitch (the following are my personal observations):

High pitch, generally a good sign.
Middle pitch, no major upheavals.
Lower pitch, disruption or the need for change.
Very low, disturbing pitch – a sign of illness, bad luck, or ill-intent.

Consider tempo and rhythm. If you hear isolated notes, with no discernible pattern, this is probably an issue that is "potential" rather than existent. If you hear a clear, symmetrical pattern, it is probably an ongoing issue, an established situation. If you hear a jarring, or broken, changeable rhythm, you are dealing with disruption, intrusion, someone else's hand at work. Slower notes or melodies are usually beneficial, as are jaunty ones, with consistent speed. What denotes issues is a changeable tempo, something that chops and switches.

# Chapter 13

# Hexing and Healing in Draíocht Ceoil

In Ireland, the ability to hex and heal have always been flip sides of the same coin. We know quite a lot about the history and use of both from a wide variety of sources e.g. the Old Irish texts including Law texts and religious writings, folklore collections and contemporary accounts. People outside of Irish culture are often surprised by how cursing and ill-wishing existed hand in hand with devout religious beliefs even today. As mentioned before, an oppressed people turn to whatever delivers justice when denied it by the State. Hexing is a route to natural justice, to redressing wrongs and resolving situations where there is an imbalance of power. Ill-wishing is viewed with more disapprobation, as something mean spirited and spiteful. A person might hex someone who did wrong to them and remain respectable but to ill-wish out of spite threatened the peace of the community. There are many remedies for ill-wishes, and local wise woman would regularly have been asked to intervene, but a justified hex was unbreakable, unless the target performed some form of penitence.

Hexing finds its roots in the *Filí* and their tradition of satire, especially their privilege to level criticism at those in power, but it would be wrong to assume that it was only used for such lofty purposes. Ordinary people also had their curses, just as they had their charms. As we travel forward in time from the pre-Christian and Early Medieval periods, we see some of the forms and techniques of the Satirist enter the practices of folk magic, notably the use of repetition, poetic forms, nonsense words, and the way in which curses are performed.

Satire did not mean (generally speaking) what we would mean by the word now – although there are similarities. In

Irish, satire or *Aer* is the opposite of *Molad* (praise), and it was primarily used by the poets to enforce their own or their patrons' claims to rights and privileges. As such, it was taken very seriously indeed and was greatly feared. This power was important to the status of poets and meant they were treated with respect. The power they wielded was not merely political but was absolutely held to be magical – the results of the successful satire were tangible, made manifest in this physical reality. The most famed manifestation was the three blemishes that could be raised on the subject's cheek but in one case the very walls of Tara fell.

The flip side was that to wield *Aer* without just cause would ensure penalties for the poet. These ranged from being marked magically themselves, to the victim extracting their full honour price for slander under Brehon Law. In the *Book of Ballymote,* a treatise entitled *"Cis Lir Fodla Aire*?" ("How many forms of satire are there?") answers its own question with the following: *"Ni hansa. A tri .i. aisnes ocus ail ocus aircetal"* (Not hard, three – declaration, insult, incantation."

*Aisnes Aire,* the first of these, is translated as "without rhyme"- this includes nonsense words, or a straightforward declaration or statement without poetic form, although not without wit. These were insults that conformed more or less to set phrases – the ideal insult for every occasion! While not the most elaborate or esoteric way to hex, it was valued enough to be recorded and was considered effective in a blunt, unvarnished way.

This is distinct from the *Ail,* the ability to raise the blemishes that shame the wrongdoer, but again is rendered in several texts as not necessarily being "rhymed". There is a suggestion of on-the-spot composition, a sharp-witted riposte to insults or dishonour. *Imbas* plays a significant role in Ail, the ability to compose in the moment and to deliver a sharp rebuke. Firenne (Truths) is the basis of the *Ail* form, and if the satire is unjust the poet is the one who suffers.

The third, *Aircetal Aire,* is the full poetic arsenal of satire, from innuendo to full satire, comprising ten categories in all. Three of these categories relate to satire done in secret, whether the poet hides their activity, or the subject is not explicitly named. While the political power of the poet lay in public performance of their duties, their magical power was wielded both publicly and privately in equal measure. The secretive nature of some of their powers added to their status in society. Interestingly, this is echoed in later Irish folk stories, where the subject of a hex does not need to know they were hexed for the spell to be effective – the source of sudden ill-fortune had to be discovered by the Bean Feasa and traced to its origins. A recurring theme in stories is a powerful hex spoken against erring landlords, who were unaware of the spell but affected by it.

Some, of the categories of satire like "Excess of Praise," are mocking while others are simply unbridled, public attacks. Overall, though, subtle attacks are very much a part of the tradition, with the *Breithe Nemed* telling us "Poets have a strange power, satire with a hint of praise and praise with a hint of satire." A double-edged sword, wielded by masters of word play.

The category that has had the greatest influence on Irish folk magic is the *Gleann Diceann* (glam dicind, in older manuscripts) defined as an endless or permanent "bite" – an incantation spell, related to the belief that a curse could raise three or one of three blemishes. Here the blemishes can be metaphorical as well as physical – the effect of the curse will be felt repeatedly, over time.

In the tract *Uairacecht na Riar,* we find the magical elements of the practice further emphasized, and of particular interest in Draíocht Ceoil is the statement that its power requires "... harmonious reciting, magical wounding, sorcery." Effective composition and delivery require a knowledge of the power of sound. The *Uairacecht Becc* also stresses the need for poets to combine skill in composition with magic, and then with "*Imbas Forosnai*" or "knowledge that illuminates" which means magical inspiration.

Some scholars argue that these requirements relate to either poetic form or magical prophetic workings but taken as a whole with other works they most likely refer to both. The status of the poet and especially their skills in satire, place them astride several roles and attribute to them both mundane and magical skills simultaneously.

The various classes of the poets were held in high or low esteem according to their rank, with some declared nuisances and others held in high regard but all were accorded a status above the norm, specifically due to the fear of satire. This power was an attribute of all the classes. Even the *Cainte,* a type described as "he who obtains his food through the threat of satire" in the *Miadshlechte,* considered on a par with the lowly bard or *fer carda,* is accorded some rights and privileges in society. To our ancestors, the magical properties of satire were so real, they found a place in the laws and regulations of the time. Examples of a typical curse in Early Irish satire is that uttered by Neide against his uncle Caiar in the *Uairacecht Becc*:

Maile, Baire, Gaire Cecht
Cot-mBeotar, Celtrai, catha Caiar
Caiar di-ba, Caiar di-ra-Caiar
Fo ro, fo mara, fo chara Caiar.

In English:

Evil death, short life to Caiar
Spears of battle will have killed Caiar
May Caiar die, may Caiar depart -Caiar
Caiar under earth, under embankments, under stones
(Breathnach, 1987)[49]

You can see clear use of repetition, strong stresses within the line on certain syllables, the name of the victim being used repeatedly, imperative language and use of present tense. As a curse this could have been composed any time in the last one thousand years, many of the same techniques being used in hexing today. Indeed the use of "may" (e.g. May Caiar die, may Caiar depart) is found in the traditional short but effective curses of more modern times, which often start "May you..." Irish curses such as "*Go dtachfadh an diabhal tú*" (may the devil choke you) or "*Go ndalladh an diabhal tú*" (may the devil blind you) are of this tradition.

In folk magic we have, besides the *Glean Diceann*, several other common curses. The most well-known are *Malachy* (generally translated simply as "curse,") *Bulan* (cursing stones) and *piseógs*. This last can be translated in several ways, as with many interesting Irish words. It can mean simply a superstition, a taboo (*Geis*) or a charm or spell. In folklore, *piseógs* are usually described as small, local mischiefs, often involving women who are held to have ill-wished an individual.

While many curses were private, secretive activities, many more were performed as public spectacles at fairs, political gatherings and other communal events. In this we can see yet another echo of the Rosc form of poetry. The Rosc being the most important poetic form of Early Irish society, used in legal and political matters, strongly influenced the way in which modern Irish folk traditions performed public hexes. Its very public, political usage evolved into the use of curses against hated British landlords and their military and legal establishments.

This is one area in which the mention of deity actually does occur, with the use of words like "Mary, Mother of God," or "Son of God," which obviously implies a hope that those entities would add power to the curse. However, it is important to recognize that in earlier times the names would have been different, evoking other deities. What remains constant is a belief in the power of words. Mingled in with the saints of Christianity were references to local legends and the Sidhe, as well as "nonsense words," akin to those used in lilting and keening. Therefore, in my opinion the use of seemingly overt religious invocation has to be taken as part of a whole – using names and words that were held to be powerful regardless of their origins.

In an echo of the Early Irish satirists, from 1700 onwards we find accounts of cursing that combine theatrics, poetic language, drama and grotesques in equal measure.[50] It becomes a tool of supernatural justice, utilizing whatever tools and imagery worked best at the time.

Certain categories of people were held to have the power of cursing, especially blacksmiths and millers. Curses involved the use of their anvil or millstone, and the National Folklore Collection records hint that the curse was a specific format, the words a closely guarded secret and the anvil or stone was involved in the performance of the malediction. The sound of this being struck was inherently magical. As mentioned before, landlords were increasingly the target of curses, some very successful, and it is clear from the Folklore collection that desperate times provoked an equally desperate response.

Priests and saints were equally quick to curse, often gruesomely, and this in turn increased their status among the populace. The tradition of attributing curses to saints has continued into the modern era, with the story of the heart of St Laurence O'Toole. The 800-year-old relic was stolen from Christ Church Cathedral. Because of the vagaries of Irish history, the relic was housed in the Church of Ireland cathedral and stolen from there by unknown thieves in 2012. After six years it was returned, because the thieves said it was cursed, and caused heart attacks among their families.[51]

While the Church outlawed cursing by priests as early as 1798, it continued into the twentieth century. Perhaps the most famous modern curse is that placed on the unfortunate Mayo GAA football team. On the 23rd of September 1951, Mayo won the All-Ireland senior football championship final, triumphing over Meath in Croke Park stadium in Dublin. The entire county was plunged into celebration with the victorious team at the centre of the revelries. Accounts vary slightly, but the core of the story is that they offended a priest, by failing to show respect as they passed a funeral in Oxford. The priest cursed them saying, "For as long as you all live, Mayo won't win another All-Ireland."

They have reached eleven finals and counting but have been defeated in each. The last member of the fateful team, Paddy Prendergast, passed away in September 2021 so it remains to be seen if Mayo will now emerge from the curse.

An interesting modern curse is known as the *Caip Bháis*. This originates from the humble candle snuffer, a household object, (also associated with the "Black Cap" worn by English Judges to deliver death sentences) and this association with "extinguishing" lent its name to a death curse. It later entered English as "kibosh" as in to stop something (put the kibosh on it).

In earlier times, the performance of a curse was associated with ritualistic actions. The corrguinecht is often translated as Crane Killing (also Heron killing) or crane-wounding, and is a spell chanted while standing on one leg, with one arm behind the back or outstretched, and one eyed closed. (This crane pose is not limited to the corrguinecht alone, it is also recorded in other circumstances. Lugh adopts it to deliver a Rosc of praise). In folk magic, curses were done in public as well as in private, and public curses utilized ritualistic and poetic language, and actions (e.g. striking the anvil, beating the ground with sticks, turning the millstone and so on).

Words, rhythms, tempo and volume are all important in the art of hexing. Above all, it is vital to be clear in intention, to have (or at least, be convinced you have) right on your side and to avoid a scattergun approach. Cursing in Irish culture was colourful, almost playful in its word play, but was a deadly serious tool in the hands of an oppressed populace.

Hexing utilizes lilting and nonsense words as well as words of power; folk tales recount the person cursing, usually a woman, muttering under her breath, and using words they couldn't identify. If some curses drew their power from public performance and announcing intent to your community, others drew power from cloaking the intent, hinting at the fact without revealing the specifics. One assumes an element of plausible deniability was also at play – if you couldn't recount what was said, you couldn't prove that you were in fact cursed. It also echoes the categories of satire from Early Irish sources – a mix of public and clandestine.

## Hexing *Bodhrán*

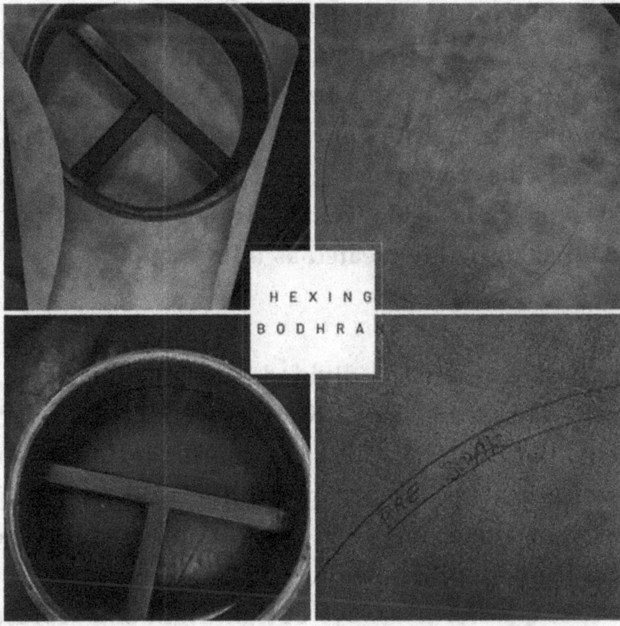


HEXING BODHRÁN IN CONSTRUCTION

The *Bodhrán* is a fixed frame tambour drum used in Irish Traditional Music, played with a stick called a *cipín*. Part of the history of the *Bodhrán* is its duality of purpose. It was used as a practical farming implement, a winnower, then covered in goat skin to be used as a musical instrument. In a time of scarce resources access to dedicated musical instruments was rare and they were prized. Only a few owned fiddles, and they were often quite crudely made. Harps had long passed into the hands of the elite, and the majority of favoured instruments were things like spoons that could be used for rhythm and then replaced in a drawer to be used for dinner. To take a *Bodhrán* and dedicate it to one use was a rare and serious thing. A hexing *Bodhrán* was not a common implement, but it existed to be used in serious situations of public interest. It was a tool created to be used by one person, which in itself was rare.

The construction of a Hexing drum is complex, and I do a comprehensive outline in my class with the Irish Pagan School "Hexing and Warding," but to give a short overview – A *bodhrán* is skinned with goat skin, which has a vellum-like surface. You can buy a pre-made drum, but make sure it is a traditionally made, handmade instrument and preferably Irish made. These are relatively inexpensive.

Goat skin lends itself well to drawing/decorating. On the surface three layers are created as follows.

### *First Layer*

The drum surface area is divided into four quarters. Around the outer edge of the skin, I draw a decorative border, which represents the Boundary. In each quarter I draw a symbol or write words that represent a particular aspect – starting from bottom right quadrant and going around clockwise. Each quadrant has a specific role.

The first Quarter is always bottom right and represents the personal. In my example, I use the word BRAN in Ogham, the

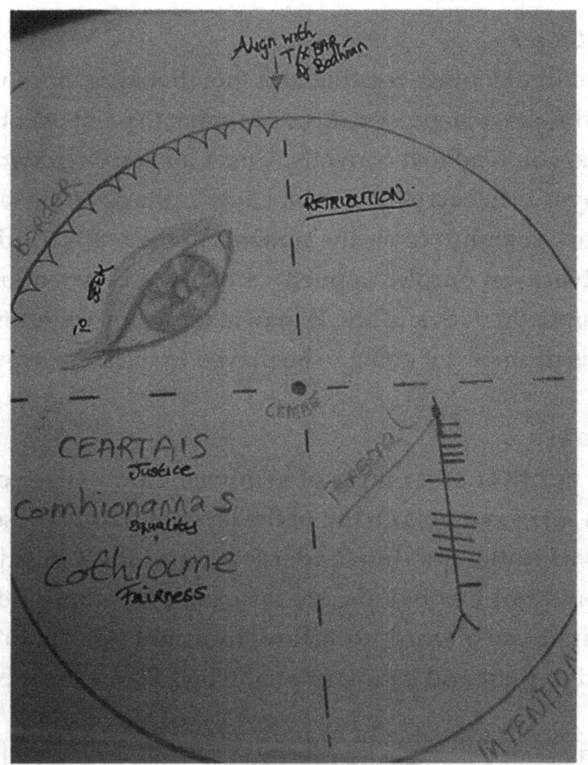


FIRST LAYER – SYMBOLS (PHOTO GMD 2023)

word meaning raven, and the root of the Clan Byrne. You must find symbols and words that mean something to you.

The second Quarter used words or symbols meaning Justice Equality and Fairness. I use the Irish words for the same in the example above.

The third Quarter used words or symbols that represent Seeking. Seeking refers to finding out the source of malice or injustice, seeking out the person responsible, the machinations behind their actions or the truth of a situation.

The fourth quarter is Retribution. You must use a very personal private word or symbol. This is why I don't give an example. You need to seek *Imbas* and try to find something you connect with deeply.

### *Second Layer*

After careful planning, creating and intentionality, once you have finished the above steps – you are now going to paint over the entire thing. Yes, you read that correctly. Cover all your hard work. I use ink on Layer 1, and acrylic paint on Layer 2 (the covering layer) You need a dark colour to cover the symbols underneath. Traditionally we use black or purple, applied carefully and intentionally, to create a smooth, dark surface. It may take several coats and that is okay. This drum is not going to be played in the usual way.

### *Third Layer*

Now we apply another layer of symbols. Using silver or white, we add a set of symbols on top of the layer of paint. These should correspond to the quarters underneath and their meaning. But they should not be obvious, so, for example, where I drew the eye, I might use a word, to mean "foresight" or "map" Again, you need to plan and be intentional. Here is one example:

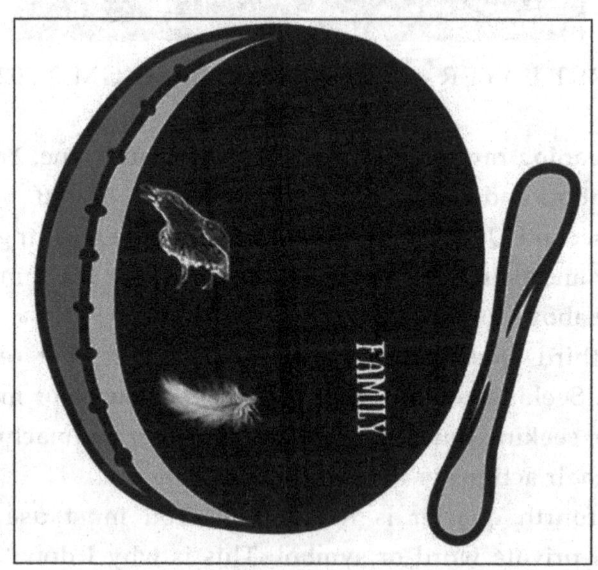


THIRD LAYER, SYMBOLS THAT ARE VISIBLE TO THE PUBLIC. (IMAGE © GMB 2023)

This is a brief outline, but it should give you an idea. Creating a magical tool of this type requires commitment, intentionality and individuality. This means the instrument is very intensely linked to you. As a result, the use of the *Bodhrán* for hexing should be carefully planned, based on a sincere desire for justice and not done in spite.

The note of the drum is also important. A lot is written about *Bodhráns* and pitch and as a player, I can tell you most of it is inaccurate. *Bodhrán*s have a natural pitch, because they are made with natural materials and while you can alter it to some degree, it will continue to return to that pitch. Smaller drums have a higher pitch, larger ones tend towards a lower pitch. Deep rims and heavier rims can help a lower pitch, but it is the skin – quality, tautness – that will have the final say. If you have to rub a lot of oils into the skin to loosen it, you are not going to be able to paint over it. So ideally go for a 16″ or 14″ drum with a good, resonant note and avoid very cheap or plastic skins. For hexing a deep note is preferred and you can use a fluffy headed or cloth covered beater to soften the note. What will be most important is using it in a rhythmic way. As you pronounce your Rosc or curse, you will use the *Bodhrán* to emphasize words, to mark the beginning and end, to rise towards an emotional crescendo and so on.

The flip side of hexing is healing, and while not as traditional, you can, of course, create a drum to be used in healing, applying the same basic layering principles above.

## Healing through Sound

Singing works extremely well in healing, especially extemporaneous chants or lullabies with "nonsense words". Nonsense words are non-lexical sounds, many of which have inherent power, and they are found in many types of folk music. Lilting is the most common form in Irish music and in Draíocht

Ceoil. It is used to heal both physical and emotional wounds, often accompanied by the *bodhrán*.

In early chapters we looked at the effect of sound on the brain, on memory, and on physiological reactions to sound, especially music. Our emotional reaction to sound is an especially important element in healing. Even listening to a favourite piece can release dopamine, while the sound of familiar voices or music can calm and reassure patients, even those in comas. A review of over 400 studies has demonstrated strong evidence of all the above, and in addition, that rhythm (rather than melody) can promote pain relief. Chanting is also particularly well suited to healing, as are gentle songs.

In Draíocht Ceoil the sound is the both the vehicle – sending intent to heal – and the tool -using sounds and words designed to have inherent healing power. Using specific words including the person's name, the ailment or complaint, the underlying cause and so on, really helps to concentrate magical energy on the person's needs. But there are other sound elements to consider.

*Isteach* (In) Pain has a sound. Physically, we associate certain sounds with pain and illness both metaphorically e.g. a wound throbbing, head thumping or literally e.g. crying with pain, moaning, sharp exclamations of pain, gasps, shortness of breath and so on. We scream if physical pain becomes unbearable, and we also scream to express emotional and psychological pain.

By using these sounds that are naturally associated with the complaint, you have a starting point to raise the magical energy needed to change the sufferer's reality. But before attempting to recreate them, we need to sit with them. Sounds associated with pain make us uncomfortable, a natural emotional response to another's suffering as well as a symptom of our own fears surrounding illness and pain. It is important to explore our discomfort to be effective healers. *Isteach* in this context includes meditating on these sounds, what they represent and how we react to them.

*Amach* (Out) – We have many sounds that we associate with healing, especially vocally. We use soothing words; we comfort and reassure. Consider a mother to a hurt child, crooning *"sokay, sokay, purpet,"* What on the surface may sound like nonsense words make sense when you realize she is murmuring "It's okay, It's okay, poor pet." Stock phrases such as "there, there, there…" seem comically cliched but we use versions of this all the time, when someone is hurt or upset.

When attempting to soothe someone who is agitated, frightened or in pain, we unconsciously follow a pattern. Initially we match their tempo – we rush to them, we hold them saying quickly, "What happened, are you okay?" and we find ourselves murmuring quickly things like "no, no, no," or similar. This mirroring of their tempo is natural, but then we do something that is at the heart of Draíocht Ceoil – we use our voices and sounds to bring down their tempo, to soothe agitation, to help them cope with pain or fright. We slow our rhythm and pace, we drop to a soothing pitch, we start to croon.

Staccato gives way to Largo. "My poor pet" "Hush now" and "Poor, poor love," we soothe. Their breathing slows, their heart rate drops, their agitation is stilled. If they are injured, we can begin to examine the wound. Often a hurt person is afraid to let their injury be touched, in the initial moments of pain and confusion. We signal that we can be trusted to be gentle by displaying calming, slow paced, medium to lower pitch tones. And vitally, we change their reactions and feelings in the process. Ideally, we want to turn the sounds associated with pain into ones associated with healing. The same basic principles apple to healing both immediate injury or pain, and long-term illness.

The first step in healing is consent. Do not attempt to heal people without talking to them and understanding their needs because illness is a complex situation, physically and emotionally. Sometimes the help people need is not the help we think they need – a useful thing to bear in mind in both mundane and magical situations. If someone wants your healing, ask them what that means to them. Simple requests would be relief from pain, comfort, easing of symptoms but more nuanced are requests to help with the psychological trauma of illness and pain. As someone with a life-shortening autoimmune disease, I can put up with any amount of physical hardships and side effects of medication but the reality of probably not living to see my young children grow into full adulthood is far harder to bear. My healing has revolved around that, not physical symptoms. Hope – of a cure, or more effective treatment or perhaps just beating the odds – is a double-edged sword and there is no room in Irish traditions for false promises, snake oil and egotistical delusions of curing serious illnesses through solely magical means.

One issue of consent that is very difficult to resolve is dementia related illnesses. Obviously, the impulse to try to help a loved one with the same is very strong and consent is often almost impossible to obtain in any meaningful way. In these circumstances, ask yourself – if the person was fully aware, what would they want? Did they prior to their illness believe in or request magical healing? If the answer is yes, then the next issue is what form of healing? No amount of magical intent will reverse dementia. But there are two safe lines of actions – one, to promote a sense of calm and well-being in the person (which in turn alleviates a lot of the associated issues of dementia) and two, to see if those caring for the person need or want healing. Often it is family carers who could do with help.

Having established consent, the next step is to know what form of healing they require. In order to have a clear intent and purpose for your working, be as specific as possible. Even if someone asks in a loose sort of way, "I want to feel better," drill down a little – do they need more energy or relief from pain?

To build a healing I usually start with music, following the principle of matching the "sound" of their current situation. Pain from a chronic, long-term illness is not something that will peak and then pass. It is a constant unwelcome visitor in their lives. I try to find a way to express this through sound. It is helpful to get the subject to choose a piece of music to express their pain. Often even those who are not into the genre turn to classical music – Tchaikovsky's Symphony No 6, Pathétique, was chosen by a friend who is a heavy metal fan. They immediately responded to its dignified, and sombre low tones and its air of weary sadness but lack of sentimentality or flashy techniques. At intervals the ominous roll of the timpani adds to the feeling that under even the more soothing passages there lurks pain and there is a sense of gentle, dogged endurance.

But as the violins soar in the melody around fifteen minutes in, there is a perfect moment to move into a different mood. I didn't tell them where I was taking it – the burst into the joy and enthusiasm of Prokofiev's "Classical" Symphony with its whimsy and insistent tempo actually made them laugh out loud. Obviously not every working is done with the person present, but it is always worth involving them as much as possible and to remember that joy and laughter heal.

As an aside, modern technology makes it easier to use music, to combine pieces and to access genres with which you might not be familiar. Taking time to explore diverse genres and note your emotional reaction is a great way to deepen your understanding of Draíocht Ceoil.

Healing is reinforced by the use of words, and while I do use non-lexical sounds, mainly to express either the pain itself or to represent soothing, the main weight of the work rests on carefully constructed verse. I don't follow the strict rules of any one Irish poetic form, but I do create within the same tradition including using internal rhyme, alliteration and stresses, using the present tense, using the technique of *Dúnadh* (opening and closing lines the same or strongly echoing each other).

If you would like to try to write using a traditional Irish poetic form, I recommend the *Dechnad Cummaisc* which uses four-line stanzas. There are eight syllables in the first and third lines. There are four syllables in the second and fourth lines, which both end-rhyme with each other and the final word of line three rhymes with the middle of line four. Purely personal UPG, I find this form works very well for many workings.

The other useful form – especially for complex workings – is the *Droigneach*. This consists of quatrains, but they can be combined to form longer stanzas. Each line can be anything between 9 to 13 syllables as long as you remain consistent. The first and third lines, and second and fourth lines, rhyme. Each couplet (e.g. lines one to two, three to four) contains an internal rhyme and heavy alliteration. The final word of each line has three syllables and in a subtle *Dúnadh,* the last syllable of the poem rhymes with the first syllable.

Even if you prefer simpler or less rigidly constructed verse, it is a great exercise to try each of these forms, as well as the Rosc, to get a sense of the rigours employed by the *Filí* in their art. It can be an act of devotion and respect to the Irish tradition, and the value lies in the attempt rather than the result.

Having created the musical background to the working and composed the verse containing the intent, tying it to the subject and stating the desired outcome, I like to mark the beginning and end of the working with a specific sound. For healing, I use high pitched Tibetan Cymbals, and for hexing, my Hexing *Bodhrán*. For cleansing spaces, I use timpani and cymbals and whistles, for divination I use long, low, soothing notes. This acts to reinforce the *Dúnadh,* the closing of the working in its own loop.

Performance of a healing spell is dependent on the circumstances. If you are asked to do it at a bedside obviously it will play out differently than at home in your own space. You can invite the subject to witness via video call, or record it for them, or perform it privately – adjust your performance to the situation.

The act of healing is not an easy one, and you should be careful to set boundaries around yourself, for example, create a ward to hold in your hand while doing the healing work. Also use sound energy to cleanse your space when finished. I find that ending any healing work with soothing, gentle music at a low volume helps both the recipient and me to "wind down," after the effort. Another helpful tip is to leave them with a song, or piece of music, which represents the ongoing healing. Encourage them to play it and listen to it regularly – daily, if possible – and to set aside that time to reinforce their desire to heal and to feel better mentally and physically. Don't forget, this can be a joyous upbeat piece as well as a soothing one. Laughter, after all, is a great medicine.

### *Exercise*

A very useful tip is to have "tools" for healing set up, ready to use. For example, dedicate a particular item, preferably a small musical instrument (e.g. a handheld cymbal, a drum, or a rattle) and choose a piece that represents healing (or compose one). Write a poem of healing – you need to keep it generic as you are creating a tool rather than healing a specific complaint). The intent is to imbue the item with healing power. You can, of course, do more than one item at a time. Set out your intent, layer the words over the piece of music, and "soak" the item in the energy you raise. Remember to "open" and "close" the working. Here is an example of one I tend to do.

I play the music in the background, meditating on the intent, and consciously raise the energy from the sound. I place the actual spoken part of the working in the middle of the piece of music, so that not only does it open and close with words, the opening and ending of the music reinforce that. At the roughly halfway mark I recite my poem three times.

In this maker of sound
carrier of note, messenger
of intent, we find the power
of healing, of easing, of
gentleness, it is the soft
breeze bringing comfort,
it is the warm ray of sun
and the cool water of the stream
and it has all the power of
*Suantraí*, the joy of *Geantraí*
the empathy of *Goltraí*
as one, as one purpose
in this maker of sound

And then I continue to meditate on the intent until the end of the piece.

The item can then be placed in a safe spot and used when needed. You should renew the intent as above after each use. A tool used repeatedly for any purpose gains more and more over time and usage.

This chapter concludes our journey through the magical tradition of Draíocht Ceoil. I hope that you find something within these pages to inspire and enrich your practice. I have listed valuable and trusted resources in the last chapter.

Wherever you are on your journey, I hope it brings you to a place of joy.

# Glossary

*Adh / Mí-adh / Droch-adh* – Luck /Misfortune/Bad Luck

*Áer* – Satire, the poetry of censure

*Amach* – Out, Outside. Used in Draíocht Ceoil to denote making sound, externalising

*Bard* – a subsection of *Filí*, an accompanist to the *Filí*

*Bean Caoine* – Keening Woman

*Bean Feasa* – Wise woman

*Birach Bríathar* – Sharp with Words, another name for a Satirist

*Bodhrán* – traditional Irish fixed frame tambour drum, usually made of ash and goatskin

*Breacc* – One of the Three Strains of Poetry, Speckled or Mixed poetry

**Bréága** – Lies

*Brí* – Wild natural energy

*Bua* – energy derived from human activity or usage

*Cairdeas* **-Friendship**

*Caoin, Caoin***te** – The Keen, Keening, the lament for the dead

*Cara, Mo Chara* – Friend, My Friend

**Consaint** – Protection

*Draoí* – Magic

*Dubh* – One of the Three Strains of Poetry, Black or Satire/Hex poetry

*Dúnadh* – Closing, to open and close a poem with the same line

**Fáilte** – Welcome

*Filí* – Poet, one of the highest classes in Old Irish Society

*Find* – One of the Three Strains of Poetry, White or Praise poetry

**Galar** – Disease

*Geantraí* – One of the Three Strains of Music, happy music

*Gleann Diceann* – The Endless Bite, The Hard Word, A form of Hex or Satire

*Goltraí* – One of the Three Strains of Music, Sad music

*Imbas, Imbas Forasnaí* – Inspiration
*Isteach* – In, Inside. Used in Draíocht Ceoil to denote listening, internalising
**Mheabhlaireacht** – Deception
*Nemed* – Noble, Privileged
*Ollamh* – Highest grade of *Filí*, Doctor of Literature
**Portaireacht Bhéil** – Mouth music, Lilting
*Saor* – Free Person in Old Irish Society
*Sláinte* – Health
*Suantraí* – One of the Three Strains of Music, Soothing music
**Teorainn** – Boundary
*Timpán* – ancient small instrument
*Tinneas* – Illness

# Endnotes

1 NFC 0265: 395 Thomas Kavanagh, Hacketstown, Co Carlow. Collector: Patrick O'Toole 1935.

2 NFC 0220:259 unattributed Collector: Tomás ó Ciardha (1936) Rita Mills.

3 NFC 0558: 107 Mrs Tom Foley, Derreen, Co Limerick Collector: Liam Shine (1938).

4 Free YouTube resource, which explains and demonstrates the widow key in divination. (Lora O'Brien, Geraldine Moorkens Byrne).

5 The Irish Oral Tradition and Print Culture, Hana F. Khasawneh: Studies: An Irish Quarterly Review, Vol. 103, No. 409, Changing Ireland (Spring 2014), pp. 81–91.

6 Whitley Stokes Translation, (1905).

7 Anna Remington, Jake Fairnie, A sound advantage: Increased auditory capacity in Autism, Cognition, Volume 166, 2017, Pages 459–465, ISSN 0010–0277.

The *Filí* used words as weapons, and their use of words, with many layers of meaning attached to each, was a special language understood only by the elite. Words that can have complex meanings make stronger magic. Identifying sound that has power will become easier the more you practice.

8 https://www.instagram.com/p/CNBDo8MpALr/ @NASA March 29th, 2021.

9 Deryck Cooke, (1989) *The Language of Music,* Oxford University Press.

10 Henrietta Leyser *Medieval Women, A Social History of Women in England, 450–1500*. Chapter 7.

11 Dr. Oliver Sacks (2007) *Musicophilia: Tales of Music and the Brain,* Picador.

12 University of Utah Health. "Music activates regions of the brain spared by Alzheimer's disease." ScienceDaily. ScienceDaily, 28 April 2018.

Having established that music does in fact affect us, and to an extent, why, it remains to say what practical use can be made of this knowledge as magical practitioners.

13 Wolfgang Meid, (2015) The romance of Froech and *Find*abair, or The driving of Froech's cattle: Táin bó Froích, ed. Albert Bock, Benjamin Bruch, and Aaron Griffith, Institut für Sprachen und Literaturen der Universität Innsbruck.

14 The Power of Sound: Music and Magic in Pre-Christian Irish Folklore by Heather Beltz, B.A. in Music Thesis In Musicology, Chapter 2.

15 *The Relationship between Music and the Supernatural as that is portrayed in Early Medieval Irish literature*. Karen M. O'Keefe, University of Edinburgh, 1995.

16 *Power and Christian Ethics,* Prof J.P. Mackey ISBN 13: 9780521426114 Publisher: Cambridge University Press, 2005.

17 Simon O'Dwyer, Ancient Music and Instruments of Ireland and Britain, Ancient Music of Ireland quoting Peter Holmes 1974 Thesis on Bronze Age Metalwork.

18 NFCS 0298: 037 unattributed, teacher: Na Siúracha, Convent of Mercy, Skibbereen Co. Cork collector: Eibhlín Ní Chárthaigh.

19 NFCS 1119: 201–202 Mr Kilmartin, Moville, Co Donegal. Teacher: Sr. Celestine Clarke School: Convent of Mercy, Moville (roll number 9278) Moville, Co. Donegal Collector: Rita McGowan.

20 Disc 1 track 5 The Otherworld Music and Song from Irish tradition, Uí Ógáin & Sherlock, Comhairle Bhéaloideas Éireann, 2012.

21 NFCS 1001: 111 Mathew Daly Burrenrea, Co Cavan, Teacher E. Ó Raghallaigh Virginia B, Co Cavan Collector Francis Doyle, Burrenrea Co Cavan.

22 NFCS 947: 041–2 Tom Monahan, Teacher B. Ó Mórdha, Killyfargy School, Killyfargy Co Monaghan Collector Michael Moore.

23 NFCS 0050: 0221 Teacher Séamus E. Ó *Dubh*ghaill, Sraith NPS (roll number 16623), Srah, Co Galway Collector Brigid Sullivan.

24 NFCS 211: 321 Teacher: Teacher: Pádhraic Ó Rodacháin School: Crummy (roll number 12691Crummy, Co. Leitrim Collector: Patrick Gralton.

25 NFCS 183: 281 Teacher Kathleen M Doyle Kilmorgan NPS (roll number 12444) Kilmorgan, Co. Sligo Collector James Brady.

26 NFCS 0232: Page 361–2 James Guiheen (67) Derreenine, Co. Roscommon Teacher: S. Pléimeann School: Droichead na Ceathramhna, Bridgecartron, Co. Roscommon Collector: Brian Gildea.

27 NFCS370, 92–3 Eugene Drinan (56) Knockacullata, Co. Cork Teacher: Máire, Bean Uí Fheargail School: Cnoc an Chodlata, Cill an Mhuillinn (roll number 9097) Collector: Nora Drinan.

28 NFCS 0027: Page 0104 Frank Collins Tuam, Co. Galway Teacher: an tSiúr M. Oilibhéir Clochar na Trocaire Tuam, Co. Galway Collector: Mary Coghlan Tuam, Co. Galway.

29 NFCS 0385, Page 505–6 J O'Flynn (42) Ballydulea, Co Cork Teacher: Sr M. Mc Donagh School: Clochar na Trócaire Cóbh, Co. Cork.

30 NFCS 0765, Page 308–9 Mrs Sweeney Coolcor, Co. Longford Teacher: Mrs Brady School: Bunlahy, Granard, Bunlahy, Co. Longford.

31 NFCS0037,Page159–160School:Teacher:PádraigÓDonnabháin Sean-Bhaile Mór (roll number 15817) Shanballymore, Co. Galway Collector: Patrick O' Donovan Dunmore, Co. Galway.

32 NFCS 0593, Page 371–2 Michael Clune (55) Quin, Co. Clare Teacher: Mícheál Mac Clúmháin School: Clooney, Cuinche: Clooney, Co. Clare.

33 NFCS 0455 :178 Bean Nic Ghearailt Lios an Phúca, Co. Kerry Collector: Caitlín Ní Chuinnealáin Teacher: An tSr. Aodán

School: Clochar na Trócaire (roll number 13381) Killarney, Co. Kerry.

34 Boom Chack Boom—A multimethod investigation of motor inhibition in professional drummers Lara Schlaffke, Sarah Friedrich, Martin Tegenthoff, Onur Güntürkün, Erhan Genç, Sebastian Ocklenburg 04 December 2019.

35 Eblanna Raven (2016) *Imramma*, PPP Publishing Ireland.

36 NFCS 0667: 100 Teacher: M. Ní Mhuireagain School: Darver (C)., Dundalk (roll number 10547) Darver, Co. Louth Collector: Máire Nic a Mhaighistir Readypenny, Co. Louth.

37 Eblanna Raven (2016) Imramma, PPP Publishing Ireland. With practice the magical energy within us becomes a reliable tool for Draíocht Ceoil; it not only opens us to *Imbas* from external, otherworldly sources but can also in itself provide the base note for our magical workings.

38 Sean Ó'Tuathail (1993) *The Excellence of Ancient Word: Druid Rhetorics from Ancient Irish Tales*.

39 *Diddling & Fiddling: The Importance of Vocalising European Dance Music*, Rowan Piggott.

40 *Diddling and Fiddling*, Rowan Piggott, P2.

41 *Folk Music and Dances of Ireland*, Breandán Breathnach P21 1971 Mercier Press.

42 Ó Cuirreáin, Seán, Éagóir: Maolra Seoighe 7 dúnmharuithe Mhám Trasna, (Cois Life, Dublin, 2016), p. 154; The Irish Times, 5 April 2018.

43 Kevin Duffy, *Who Were the Celts?*, Barnes & Noble Inc 2000.

44 McManus, Damian. (1991). *A guide to Ogam*, Maynooth: An Sagart.

45 Grey, E (1982) Irish Text Society.

46 Mc Laughlin, M. (2019). Keening the Dead: Ancient History or a Ritual for Today? Religions, 10(4), 235. https://doi.org/10.3390/rel10040235.

47 Mooney, James. 1888. The Funeral Customs of Ireland. I Proceedings of the American Philosophical Society.

There are many ways in which you can honour your spiritual needs using the techniques of Draíocht Ceoil, including using music to amplify your prayers. The act of composing and creating – whether for fun, or for devotional purposes or magical workings – is always valuable and the more you explore these things, the better your practice will be.

48 Donnacha Dennehy Grá agus Bás ℗ 2011 Nonesuch Records Inc.

And finally, if you are interpreting divination – e.g. reading tarot – you may find that your inspiration takes the form of verse or music. It's up to you whether you translate that into plain English or surprise your sitter with an impromptu recital. As you practice Draíocht Ceoil, an awareness of sound and music will become second nature to you and permeate every aspect of life. The more you engage, the more you will receive. Music links you to the past, present and future.

49 Breathnach, L (1987) Translation, Uairacecht Becc Page 114–5.

50 Irish Cursing and the Art of Magic, 1750–2018 Thomas Waters Past & Present, Volume 247, Issue 1, May 2020, Pages 113–149.

51 The Curse of St. Laurence O'Toole, Jesse Harrington. History Ireland Vol. 26, No. 4 (JULY/AUGUST 2018), pp. 18–21.

# Valuable Resources

## Books

The following recommendations give an overview of Irish Paganism and Folk Magic.

### Lora O'Brien

*Irish Witchcraft from an Irish Witch: True to the Heart* (2nd Edition, 2020)
*The Irish Queen Medb: History, Tradition, and Modern Pagan Practice* (2020)
*Tales of Old Ireland: Retold – Ancient Irish Stories Retold for Today* (2018)

### Jon O'Sullivan

*Tales of a Dagda Bard:* Volume One (2018) Volume Two (2020)
*Harp, Club, and Cauldron – A Harvest of Knowledge*: (Editor and Contributor, 2019)

### Eddie Lenihan

*Meeting the Other Crowd: The Fairy Stories of Hidden Ireland* 2004 by Eddie Lenihan and Carolyn Eve Green (Author)

### Morgan Daimler

*The Morrigan: Meeting the Great Queens* (2014)
*Raven Goddess: Going Deeper with the Morrigan* (2020)
*Tales of the Tuatha De Danann: A Dual Language Collection of Irish Myth* (2016)
*Cath Maige Tuired: A Full English Translation* (Irish Myth Translations) (2020)

### Michael Fortune

*The May Bush in Co Wexford* (2024)

*No Twixing or Crossing – from conversations with Traveller Women*, Bunclody (2023)

**Also**

Mael Brigde, *Brigit of Ireland, a Devotional* (2023)
Dáithí O hOgain, *The Sacred Isle: Belief and Religion in Pre-Christian Ireland* (1999)
Geraldine Stout, *Newgrange and the Bend of the Boyne* (hardcover, illustrated, 2002)
Sean Duffy, *The Concise History of Ireland* (2005)
FSL Lyons, *Ireland since the Famine* (1995)
JC Beckett, *The Making of Modern Ireland* 1603–1923 (2008)
Niall Hegarty, *The History of Ireland Book* / RTE TV Documentary (2011)

**Music Books**

Uí Ógáin & Sherlock (2012) *The Otherworld Music and Song from Irish tradition*, Comhairle Bhéaloideas Éireann, inc CDs.
Pedro De Alcantara, *The Integrated String Player*, OUP/Academic (2017)

## Music for Meditation/Journeying

Turlough O'Carolan, (O'Carolan's Farewell)
John Fields (Nocturne no 1 in E flat major)
Sean O'Riada (Mise Eireann, Mná na hEireann)
Bill Whelan (Spanish Suite)
Donnacha Dennehy "Grá agus Bás" (album)
Seek out artists like Denise Chaila, Padraig Jack, Odhran Murphy and challenge your perception of "Irish music" new and old.

## Websites

**Irish Pagan School**: An Irish organization providing a huge amount of free and paid content. Authentic scholarship and

Irish voices are prioritized, along with the best of global writing and resources https://irishpaganschool.com/

## Folklore and Living Traditions

Folklore.ie (living folklore traditions) https://www.Duchas.ie (The National Folklore Collection)

Robert Lee Bewer's simple and accessible guide to several of the Irish poetic forms https://www.writersdigest.com/poetic-asides/irish-poetic-forms

## Lilting

Eimear Arkins (Irish Lilting) & Shane Farrell (*Bodhrán*) https://www.youtube.com/watch?v=43qDQqGHQe8

## Prehistoric Music

https://www.ancientmusicireland.com/ – Prehistoric Instruments, Horns, recordings and sound library.

http://irisharchaeology.ie/2014/03/five-ancient-musical-instruments-from-ireland/

# Bibliography


Alcantara, Pedro de (2017) *The Integrated String Player* Oxford University Press/Academic

Ancient Music of Ireland Website https://www.ancientmusicireland.com/

Beltz, H (2016) *The Power of Sound: Music and Magic in Pre-Christian Irish Folklore*

Breathnach, B (1971) *Folk Music and Dances of Ireland* Mercier Press

Breathnach, L (1987) [ed. and tr.], *Uraicecht na ríar: the poetic grades in early Irish law* Dublin Institute for Advanced Studies

Cooke, D (1989) *The Language of Music* Oxford University Press

Csikszentmihalyi, M.; Csikszentmihalyi, I.S. (Eds). *Optimal Experience: Psychological Studies of Flow in Consciousness*; Cambridge University Press: Cambridge, UK, 1992

Duchas.ie The National Folklore Collection, University College Dublin, Ireland

Duffy, K (2000) *Who Were The Celts*? Barnes & Noble Inc

Grey, E (1982) *Cath Maige Tuired: The Second Battle of Mag Tuired,* Irish Texts Society

Guetta, R et al. (2022) *Examining emotional functioning in Misophonia: The role of affective instability and difficulties with emotion regulation*. NIH National Library of Medicine.

Harrington, J (July/August 2018) *The Curse of St Laurence O'Toole,* History Ireland Vol. 26, No. 4

Haywood, J (2004) *The Celts: Bronze Age to New Age* Routledge

Khasawneh, H.F. The Irish Oral Tradition and Print Culture Studies: An Irish Quarterly Review, Vol. 103, No. 409, Changing Ireland (Spring 2014), pp. 81–91.

Leyser, H (1995) *Medieval Women, A Social History of Women in England,* Weidenfeld and Nicolson

Lynch, J and Wilson, C *Exploring the impact of choral singing on mindfulness*, Volume 46, Issue 6 Psychology of Music

Lyons, FSL (1985) *Ireland since the Famine*, Fontana Press

Lysaght, P (1997) *Caoineadh Os Cionn Coirp*: The Lament for the Dead in Ireland, Folklore *108*(1–2) https://doi.org/10.1080/0015587X.1997.9715938

Mackey, Prof J (2005) *Power and Christian Ethics* Cambridge University Press

McLaughlin, R (2008) *Early Irish Satire* Dublin Institute for Advanced Studies

McLaughlin, M (2019) 'Keening the Dead: Ancient History or a Ritual for Today?' *Religions*, *10*(4), 235. https://doi.org/10.3390/rel10040235

McManus, D (1991) *A guide to Ogam*. Maynooth: An Sagart

Meid, W (2015) *The romance of Froech and Findabair, or The driving of Froech's cattle: Táin bó Froích*, ed. Albert Bock, Benjamin Bruch, and Aaron Griffith, Institut für Sprachen und Literaturen der Universität Innsbruck.

Mooney, James (1888) The Funeral Customs of Ireland. I *Proceedings of the American Philosophical Society*.

Ó Bharáin, L *Bodhrán: its origin, meaning and history* Treoir vol. 39, no 4 (2007), pp. 50–6

Ó Cuirreáin, Seán, *Éagóir: Maolra Seoighe 7 dúnmharuithe Mhám Trasna*, (Cois Life, Dublin, 2016), p. 154; *The Irish Times*, 5 April 2018.

Ó Crualaoich, G (Apr., 2005) 'Reading the *Bean Feasa*' Folklore Vol. 116, No. 1 pp. 37–50

O'Dwyer, S (2004) *Ancient Music and Instruments of Ireland and Britain*, Ancient Music of Ireland

O'Keefe, K (1995) *The Relationship between Music and the Supernatural as that is portrayed in Early Medieval Irish literature* University of Edinburgh

Ó'Tuathail, S (1993) *The Excellence of Ancient Word: Druid Rhetorics from Ancient Irish Tales* Kellnhauser

Piggott, R (2018) *Diddling & Fiddling: The Importance of Vocalising European Dance Music*

Raven, E (2016) *Immrama* PPP Publishing

Remington, Dr. A and Fairnie, Dr. J *A sound advantage: Increased auditory capacity in autism*, Cognition, Volume 166, 2017, Pages 459–465, ISSN 0010–0277

Sacks, Dr O (2007) *Musicophilia: Tales of Music and the Brain*, Picador

Schlaffke et al *Boom Chack Boom—A multimethod investigation of motor inhibition in professional drummers* 04 December 2019 Brain Behav. 2020 Jan;10(1): e01490.

Swedo SE, Baguley DM, Denys D, et al. Consensus Definition of Misophonia: A Delphi Study. *Front Neurosci*. 2022; 16:841816. doi:10.3389/fnins.2022.841816

Takemitsu, T (1962, 2001) "Nature and Music" *The Book of Music and Nature: An Anthology of Sounds, Words, Thoughts*, Wesleyan University Press

Uí Ógáin, Prof R, and Sherlock, T (2012) *The Otherworld: Music and Song from Irish Tradition* Comhairle Bhéaloideas Éireann/ Four Courts Press

University of Utah Health. *Music activates regions of the brain spared by Alzheimer's disease*. ScienceDaily, 28 April 2018.

Welch, R (1996) *The Oxford companion to Irish literature*

Waters, T (2020) *Irish Cursing and the Art of Magic, 1750–2018* Past & Present, Volume 247, Issue 1

# About the Author

Geraldine Moorkens Byrne is a poet, writer and educator from Dublin, Ireland. She was a founding editor of the *Pagan Poetry Pages*. She has facilitated workshops and creative writing groups, and her work has been published in a variety of media from print anthologies to Ezines. Several poems have been performed as theatre in Ireland, the UK and USA. She was a prizewinner in the Inaugural John Creedon Listowel Writers Festival Competition. Her short story *A Stranger Among Friends,* was a winner in the Cunningham Short Story Competition. She is also the author of a popular series of mystery novels. Her collection of poetry, *Dreams of Reality,* is in its second edition.

She was the fourth generation of Byrnes to run the famous Charles Byrne Music Shop, in Stephen Street, Dublin, Ireland. This was a landmark business in the city until her retirement in 2021 and she comes from a storied family of luthiers and musicians. She is a *Bodhrán* player and singer. She currently teaches classes online, for the Irish Pagan School. Geraldine writes ceremonies and facilitates Life Rites through her website *CelebratingWords.Com* including weddings, funerals and naming ceremonies.

**From the Author**

Thank you for purchasing *Draíocht Ceoil*. My sincere hope is that you derived as much from reading this book as I did in creating it. If you have a few moments, please feel free to add your review of the book to your favorite online site. Also, if you would like to connect with my other books that are coming out in the near future, please visit my website for news on upcoming works, for recent blog posts and to sign up for my newsletter: *CelebratingWords.Com*

Sincerely, Geraldine Moorkens Byrne

## MOON BOOKS

PAGANISM & SHAMANISM

**What is Paganism? A religion, a spirituality, an alternative belief system, nature worship? You can find support for all these definitions (and many more) in dictionaries, encyclopaedias, and text books of religion, but subscribe to any one and the truth will evade you. Above all Paganism is a creative pursuit, an encounter with reality, an exploration of meaning and an expression of the soul. Druids, Heathens, Wiccans and others, all contribute their insights and literary riches to the Pagan tradition. Moon Books invites you to begin or to deepen your own encounter, right here, right now.**

**If you have enjoyed this book, why not tell other readers by posting a review on your preferred book site.**

## Bestsellers from Moon Books

**Keeping Her Keys**

An Introduction to Hekate's Modern Witchcraft

Cyndi Brannen

*Blending Hekate, witchcraft and personal development together to create a powerful new magickal perspective.*

Paperback: 978-1-78904-075-3 ebook 978-1-78904-076-0

**Journey to the Dark Goddess**

How to Return to Your Soul

Jane Meredith

*Discover the powerful secrets of the Dark Goddess and transform your depression, grief and pain into healing and integration.*

Paperback: 978-1-84694-677-6 ebook: 978-1-78099-223-5

**Shamanic Reiki**

Expanded Ways of Working with Universal Life Force Energy

Llyn Roberts, Robert Levy

*Shamanism and Reiki are each powerful ways of healing; together, their power multiplies. Shamanic Reiki introduces techniques to help healers and Reiki practitioners tap ancient healing wisdom.*

Paperback: 978-1-84694-037-8 ebook: 978-1-84694-650-9

**Southern Cunning**

Folkloric Witchcraft in the American South

Aaron Oberon

*Modern witchcraft with a Southern flair, this book is a journey through the folklore of the American South and a look at the power these stories hold for modern witches.*

Paperback: 978-1-78904-196-5 ebook: 978-1-78904-197-2

**Bestsellers from Moon Books**
**Pagan Portals Series**

**The Morrigan**
Meeting the Great Queens
Morgan Daimler
*Ancient and enigmatic, the Morrigan reaches out to us. On shadowed wings and in raven's call, meet the ancient Irish goddess of war, battle, prophecy, death, sovereignty, and magic.*
Paperback: 978-1-78279-833-0 ebook: 978-1-78279-834-7

**The Awen Alone**
Walking the Path of the Solitary Druid
Joanna van der Hoeven
*An introductory guide for the solitary Druid, The Awen Alone will accompany you as you explore, and seek out your own place within the natural world.*
Paperback: 978-1-78279-547-6 ebook: 978-1-78279-546-9

**Moon Magic**
Rachel Patterson
*An introduction to working with the phases of the Moon, what they are and how to live in harmony with the lunar year and to utilise all the magical powers it provides.*
Paperback: 978-1-78279-281-9 ebook: 978-1-78279-282-6

**Hekate**
A Devotional
Vivienne Moss
*Hekate, Queen of Witches and the Shadow-Lands, haunts the pages of this devotional bringing magic and enchantment into your lives*
Paperback: 978-1-78535-161-7 ebook: 978-1-78535-162-4

YouTube